THE GUITAR
4 Chord Songbook

PLAY 50 GREAT SONGS WITH ONLY 4 EASY CHORDS

ISBN 978-1-4803-9971-6

HAL•LEONARD®

Visit Hal Leonard Online at
www.halleonard.com

Contact Us:
Hal Leonard
7777 West Bluemound Road
Milwaukee, WI 53213
Email: info@halleonard.com

In Europe contact:
Hal Leonard Europe Limited
42 Wigmore Street
Marylebone, London, W1U 2RN
Email: info@halleonardeurope.com

In Australia contact:
Hal Leonard Australia Pty. Ltd.
4 Lentara Court
Cheltenham, Victoria, 3192 Australia
Email: info@halleonard.com.au

4 Chord Songbook

PLAY 50 GREAT SONGS WITH ONLY 4 EASY CHORDS

Contents

The Boys of Summer

Words and Music by Mike Campbell and Don Henley

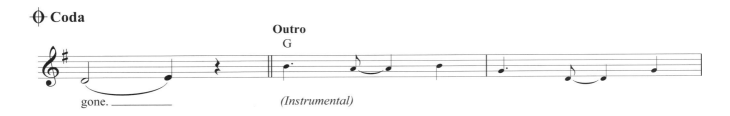

Additional Lyrics

2. I never will forget those nights. I wonder if it was a dream.
   Remember how you made me crazy? Remember how I made you scream?
   Now I don't understand what happened to our love.
   But, babe, I'm gonna get you back. I'm gonna show you what I'm made of.

Chorus: I can see you, your brown skin shinin' in the sun.
   I see you walkin' real slow and you're smilin' at everyone.
   I can tell you my love for you will still be strong
   After the boys of summer have gone.

3. Out on the road today I saw a "Deadhead" sticker on a Cadillac.
   A little voice inside my head said, "Don't look back. You can never look back."
   I thought I knew what love was. What did I know?
   Those days are gone forever. I should just let 'em go, but...

Chorus: I can see you, your brown skin shinin' in the sun.
   You got the top pulled down and radio on, baby.
   And I can tell you my love for you will still be strong
   After the boys of summer have gone.

D.S. Chorus: I can see you, your brown skin shinin' in the sun.
   You got that hair slicked back and those Wayfarers on, baby.
   I can tell you my love for you will still be strong
   After the boys of summer have gone.

Brown Eyed Girl

Words and Music by Van Morrison

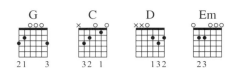

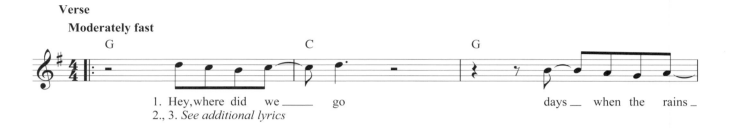

Verse
Moderately fast

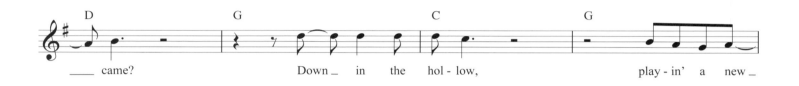

1. Hey, where did we ___ go days ___ when the rains ___
2., 3. *See additional lyrics*

___ came? Down ___ in the hol - low, play - in' a new ___

___ game, laugh - ing and a - run - ning, hey, ___ hey,

skip - ping and a - jump - ing. In the mist - y morn -

- ing fog ___ with our hearts a - thump - in', and

you, my brown eyed girl.

You, my brown eyed girl. ____ Do you re-mem-

Chorus

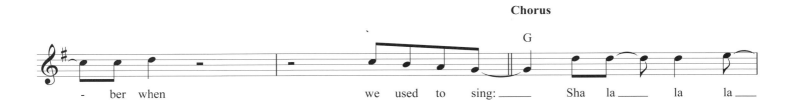

-ber when we used to sing: ____ Sha la ____ la la ____

____ la la ____ la la ____ la la la te da? ____

Sha la ____ la la ____ la la ____ la la ____ la la la te da ____

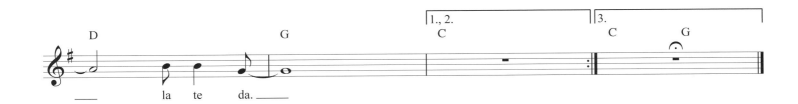

____ la te da. ____

Additional Lyrics

2. Whatever happened to Tuesday and so slow
   Going down the old mine with a transistor radio
   Standing in the sunlight laughing
   Hiding behind a rainbow's wall
   Slipping and a-sliding
   All along the waterfall
   With you, my brown eyed girl,
   You, my brown eyed girl?
   Do you remember when we used to sing:

3. So hard to find my way, now that I'm all on my own
   I saw you just the other day, my, how you have grown
   Cast my memory back there, Lord
   Sometime I'm overcome thinking 'bout
   Making love in the green grass
   Behind the stadium
   With you, my brown eyed girl
   With you, my brown eyed girl.
   Do you remember when we used to sing:

Burn One Down

Words and Music by Ben Harper

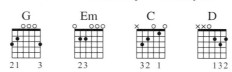

Verse
Moderately

1. Let us __ burn one from end to end, and pass it o - ver to me, __

__ my friend. _____ Burn it long, __ we'll burn it slow to light __ me up be - fore I go.

Chorus

to light __ me up be - fore I go. If you don't like __ my fi - re, then

don't come a - round, __ 'cause I'm gon - na burn one down. _____ Yes, I'm __

__ gon - na burn __ one _____ down. _____

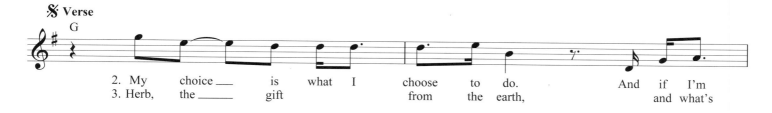

Verse

2. My choice __ is what I choose to do. And if I'm
3. Herb, the __ gift is from the earth, and what's

caus - in' no harm, ____ it should - n't both - er you. ____
from the earth ____ is of the great - est worth. ____ So be -

-fore you ____ knock it, try it first. Oh, you'll
Your choice ____ is who you choose to be. And if you're

caus - in' no harm, ____ then you're al - right with me. ____ }
see it's a bless - ing and it's not a curse. ____ } If you

Chorus

don't like ____ my fi - re, then don't come a - round, 'cause I'm ____ gon - na burn ____ one ____

To Coda ⊕

down. _____ Yes, I'm ____ gon - na burn ____ one down. ____

⊕ **Coda**

D.S. al Coda

_____ I'm gon - na burn ____ one... ____

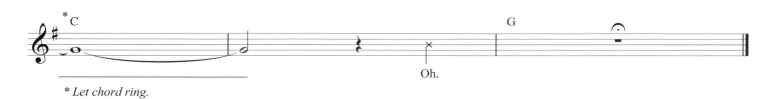

Oh.

Let chord ring.

Come On Get Higher

Words and Music by Matt Nathanson and Mark Weinberg

come on, get high-er, loos-en my lips. Faith __ and de-sire and the swing of your hips. Just

pull me down __ hard __ and drown __ me in love. __

Bridge

I miss the pull of your __ heart, I taste the sparks on your tongue.

I see an-gels and dev-ils and God __ when you come __ on, __ hold __

__ on, __ hold on, __ hold on, __ hold on. __

Outro-Chorus

Come on, get high-er, loos-en my lips. Faith __ and de-sire and the swing of your hips. Just

pull me down __ hard __ and drown __ me in love. __ So

come on, get high-er, loos-en my lips. Faith __ and de-sire and the swing of your hips. {Just
{Ev -

1.

pull me down __ hard __ and drown __ me, drown __ me in love.

2.

'ry-thing works, __ love, ev-'ry-thing works __ in your __ arms.

Cupid

Words and Music by Sam Cooke

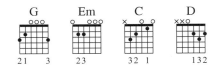

Chorus
Moderately fast

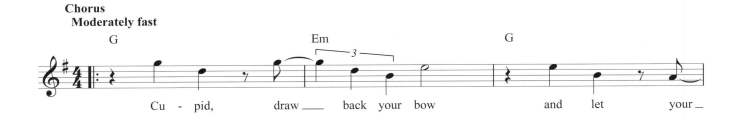

Cu - pid, draw ___ back your bow and let your ___

___ ar - row go ___ straight to my lov - er's heart for ___

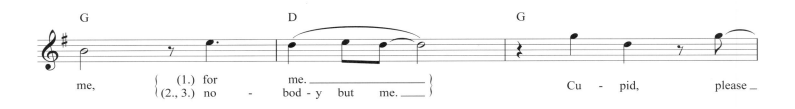

me, { (1.) for me. ___ } Cu - pid, please ___
{ (2., 3.) no - bod - y but me. ___ }

___ hear my cry and let your ___ ar - row fly ___

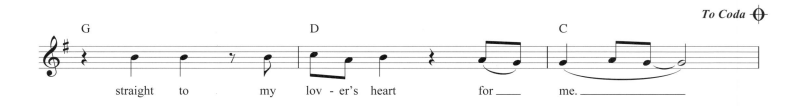

To Coda ⊕

straight to my lov - er's heart for ___ me. ___

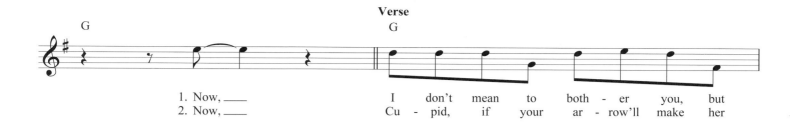

1. Now, ____ I don't mean to both - er you, but
2. Now, ____ Cu - pid, if your ar - row'll make her

I'm in dis - tress; ____ there's dan - ger of me los - ing all of
love strong for me, ____ I prom - ise I will love her un - til

my hap - pi - ness. ____ For I love a girl who does - n't
e - ter - ni - ty. ____ I know, be - tween the two of us, her

2nd time, D.C. al Coda

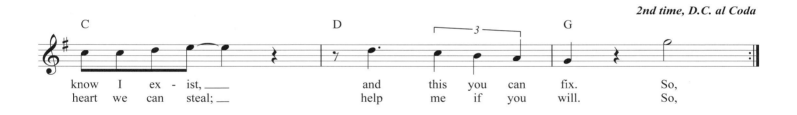

know I ex - ist, ____ and this you can fix. So,
heart we can steal; ____ help me if you will. So,

Coda

Outro

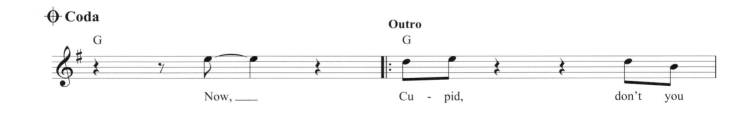

Now, ____ Cu - pid, don't you

Repeat and fade

hear me call - ing you? I need ____ you.

Every Rose Has Its Thorn

Words and Music by Bobby Dall, C.C. Deville, Bret Michaels and Rikki Rockett

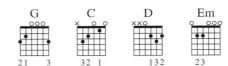

Verse
Moderately slow

1. We both lie si-lent-ly still __ in the dead of the night. __ Al-though we
2., 3. *See additional lyrics*

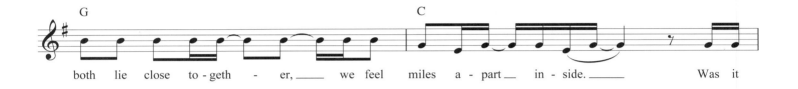

both lie close to-geth - er, _____ we feel miles a-part __ in - side. _____ Was it

some-thing I said or some-thing I did? Did my words not come out right? __ Though I

tried not to hurt __ you, _____ though I tried, but I guess that's why __ they say

Chorus

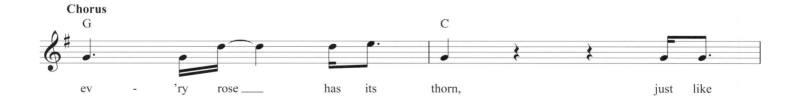

ev - 'ry rose _____ has its thorn, just like

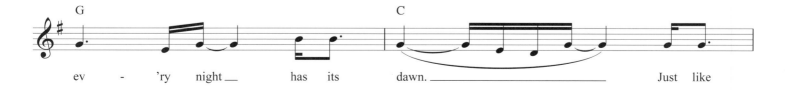

ev - 'ry night __ has its dawn. _____ Just like

ev - 'ry cow - boy _____ sings his sad, sad _____ song,

To Coda ⊕ |1.

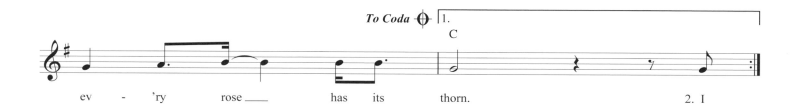

ev - 'ry rose _____ has its thorn.　　　　　　2. I

|2.　　　　　　**Bridge**

thorn.　　　　Though it's been a while _____ now, I can

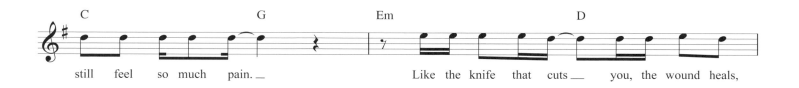

still feel so much pain. _____ Like the knife that cuts _____ you, the wound heals,

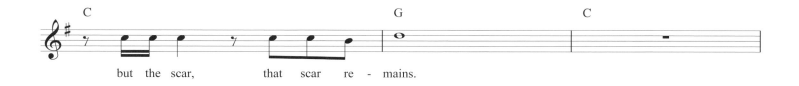

but the scar, that scar re - mains.

⊕ **Coda**

D.C. al Coda

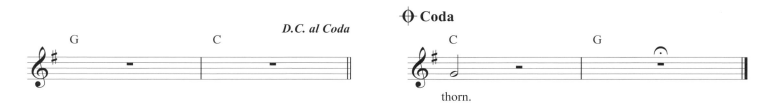

thorn.

Additional Lyrics

2. I listen to our favorite song playing on the radio,
   Hear the DJ say love's a game of easy come and easy go.
   But I wonder, does he know? Has he ever felt like this?
   And I know that you'd be here right now if I could've let you know somehow.
   I guess... *(To Chorus)*

3. I know I could have saved our love that night if I'd known what to say.
   Instead of making love, we both made our separate ways.
   And now I hear you've found somebody new and that I never meant that much to you.
   To hear that tears me up inside and to see you cuts me like a knife.
   I guess... *(To Chorus)*

Fast Car

Words and Music by Tracy Chapman

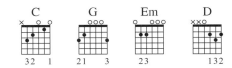

Intro
Moderately, in 2

(Instrumental)

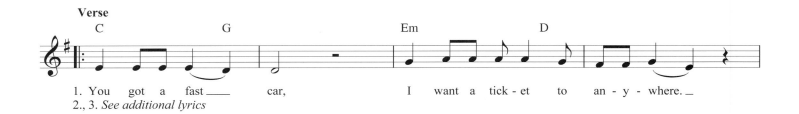

Verse

1. You got a fast ____ car, I want a tick-et to an-y-where. ____
2., 3. *See additional lyrics*

May-be we make a deal, _____ may-be to-geth-er we can get some-where. ____

An-y place is bet-ter. ____ Start-ing from ze-ro, got noth-ing to lose. ____

May-be we'll make some - thing; ____ Me, my-self, I got noth-ing to prove. ____

Play 3 times

Verse

4. You got a fast ___ car, but is it fast e - nough ___ so we can fly a - way? ___

We got - ta make a de - ci - sion: ___ leave to - night ___ or live and die this way.

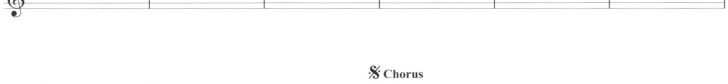

% Chorus

'Cause I re - mem - ber when we were driv - in', driv - ing in your car, ___ the

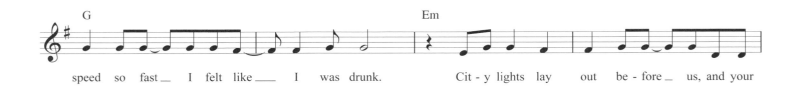

speed so fast ___ I felt like ___ I was drunk. Cit - y lights lay out be - fore ___ us, and your

arm felt nice wrapped 'round my shoul - der. And I, _____ I ___ had a

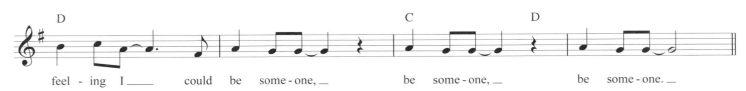

feel - ing that I ___ be - longed. ___ I, _____ I ___ had a

feel - ing I ___ could be some - one, ___ be some - one, ___ be some - one. ___

Interlude

To Coda ⊕

Verse

5. You got a fast ___ car, We go cruis - ing, en - ter - tain our - selves. ___ You
6. *See additional lyrics*

still ain't got a job, ___ and I work in a mar - ket as a check - out girl. ___

I know things ___ will get bet - ter; you'll find work, and I'll ___ get pro - mot - ed. ___

We'll move out ___ of the shel - ter, buy a big house and live in the sub - urbs. ___

___

2nd time, D.S. al Coda

'Cause I re - mem - ber when we were

⊕ Coda

Verse

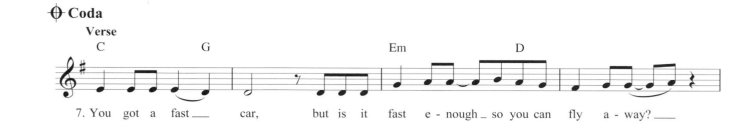

7. You got a fast____ car, but is it fast e - nough __ so you can fly a - way?____

You got - ta make a de - ci - sion: __ leave to - night __ or live and die this way.

Outro

Additional Lyrics

2. You got a fast car.
   I got a plan to get us out of here.
   I been working at the convenience store,
   Managed to save just a little bit of money.
   Won't have to drive too far,
   Just 'cross the border and into the city.
   You and I can both get jobs
   And finally see what it means to be living.

3. You see, my old man's got a problem.
   He live with the bottle, that's the way it is.
   He says his body's too old for working;
   I say his body's too young to look like his.
   My mama went off and left him;
   She wanted more from life than he could give.
   I said somebody's got to take care of him.
   So I quit school and that's what I did.

6. You got a fast car,
   And I got a job that pays all our bills.
   You stay out drinking late at the bar,
   See more of your friends than you do of your kids.
   I'd always hoped for better,
   Thought maybe together you and me would find it.
   I got no plans, I ain't going nowhere,
   So take your fast car and keep on driving.

Fidelity

Words and Music by Regina Spektor

Fifteen

Words and Music by Taylor Swift

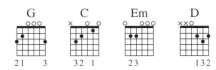

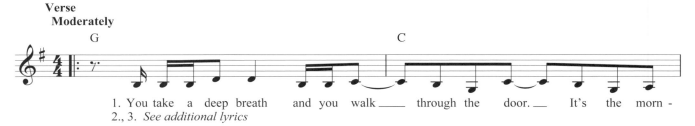

Verse
Moderately

1. You take a deep breath and you walk through the door. It's the morn-
2., 3. *See additional lyrics*

in' of your ver-y first day. You say "hi" to your friends you ain't

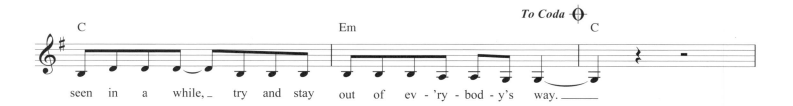

seen in a while, try and stay out of ev-'ry-bod-y's way.

It's your fresh-man year and you're gon-na be here for the next four years in this

town. Hop-in' one of those sen-ior boys will wink at you and say, "You know, I

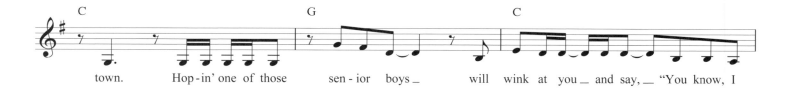

have-n't seen you a-round be-fore." 'Cause when you're

Chorus

fif-teen and some-bod-y tells you they love you, you're gon-na be-lieve

fif - teen, don't ___ for - get ___ to look ___ be - fore ___ you fall. ___

I've found time ___ can heal most ___ an - y - thing, ___ and you just might

find who you're sup - posed to be. ___ I did - n't know who I was s'posed to be ___

Outro

at fif - teen. La la la ___ la la la ___ la la ___ la la.

La la la ___ la la la, ___ your ver - y first ___ day.

Take a deep breath, girl. Take a deep breath as you walk ___ through the doors. ___

Additional Lyrics

2. You sit in class next to a redhead named Abigail,
   And soon enough you're best friends,
   Laughin' at the other girls who think they're so cool.
   We'll be outta here as soon as we can.
   And then you're on your very first date, and he's got a car,
   And you're feelin' like flyin'.
   And your mama's waitin' up, and you're thinkin' he's the one,
   And you're dancin' 'round your room when the night ends, when the night ends.

3. Back then, I swore I was gonna marry him someday,
   But I realized some bigger dreams of mine.
   And Abigail gave everything she had
   To a boy who changed his mind, and we both cried.

Follow You Down

Words and Music by Bill Leen, Phil Rhodes, Jesse Valenzuela, Robin Wilson and D. Scott Johnson

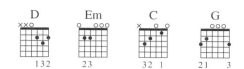

Verse
With energy

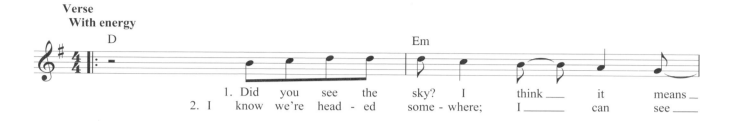

1. Did you see the sky? I think it means
2. I know we're head - ed some - where; I can see

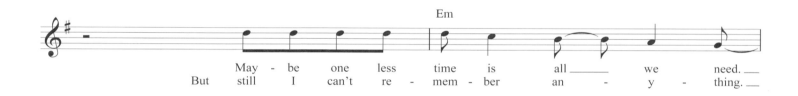

___ that we've ___ been lost. ___
___ how far ___ we've come. ___

Maybe one less time is all ___ we need. ___
But still I can't re - mem - ber an - y - thing. ___

___
___

I can't real - ly
Let's not do the

help it if ___ my tongue's ___ all tied ___ in knots. ___
wrong thing and ___ I'll swear ___ it might ___ be fun. ___

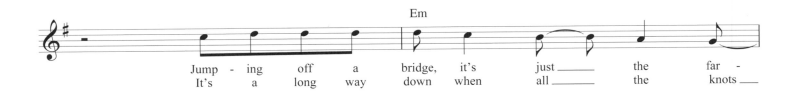

Em

Jump - ing off a bridge, it's   just ____ the far -
It's a long way down when   all ____ the knots ____

C

- thest that ____ I've ev - er been. ____
____ we've tied ____ have come ____ un - done. ____

𝄋 **Chorus**

G   Em

An - y - where you   go, ____   I'll

C   D

fol - low ____ you down, ____   an - y - place but those ____

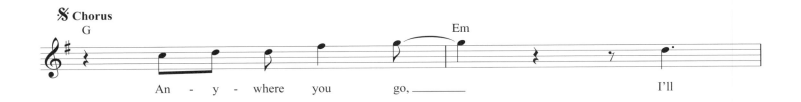

Em   C

____ I know ____ by heart. ____

G   Em   C

An - y - where you   go, ____   I'll fol - low ____ you down. ____

D

____   I'll fol - low you   down, ____

To Coda ⊕

Em   C

____ but not ____ that far. ____

26

Garden Party

Words and Music by Rick Nelson

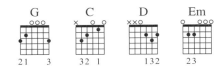

G   C   D   Em

21 3   32 1   132   23

% Verse
Moderately slow, in 2

G   C

1. I went to a gar-den par-ty,   to rem-i-
2.–4. *See additional lyrics*

G   C   G   D

nisce with my ___ old friends; ___   a chance to share ___ old mem-

Em   C   D   G

-o-ries ___   and play our songs a-gain.   When I

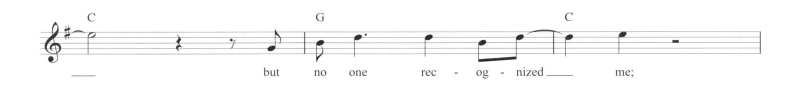

C   G

got to the gar-den par-ty,   they all knew my name, ___

C   G   C

___   but no one rec-og-nized ___ me;

                                                                        Chorus

D   G   C   D

I did-n't look the same. ___ But it's all right now, ___

I learned my les-son well. _____ You see, you

can't please ev-'ry-one, _____ so you got to please your-self. _____

To Coda ⊕

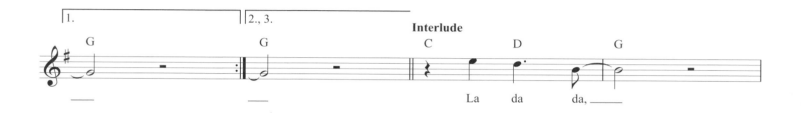

Interlude

_____ _____ La da da, _____

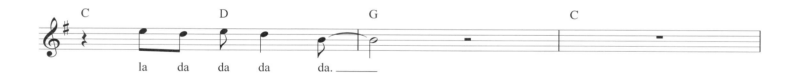

la da da da da. _____

1st time, D.S.
2nd time, D.S. al Coda

⊕ **Coda**

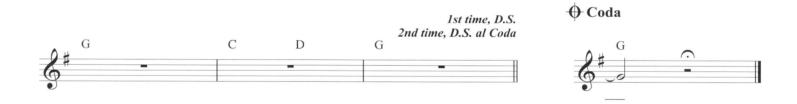

Additional Lyrics

2. People came for miles around; everyone was there.
   Yoko brought her walrus; there was magic in the air.
   And over in the corner, much to my surprise,
   Mr. Hughes hid in Dylan's shoes, wearing his disguise.

3. I played them all the old songs; I thought that's why they came.
   No one heard the music; we didn't look the same.
   I said hello to Mary Lou; she belongs to me.
   When I sang a song about a honky-tonk, it was time to leave.

4. Someone opened up a closet door and out stepped Johnny B. Goode,
   Playing guitar like a-ringin' a bell, and lookin' like he should.
   If you gotta play at garden parties, I wish you a lotta luck;
   But if memories were all I sang, I'd rather drive a truck.

Girls Just Want to Have Fun

Words and Music by Robert Hazard

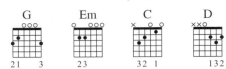

Verse
Bright Pop

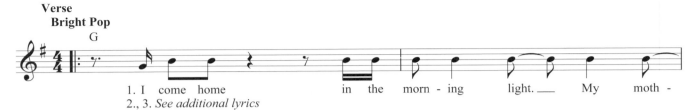

1. I come home in the morn-ing light.___ My moth-
2., 3. *See additional lyrics*

-er says, "When ___ you gon - na live your life right?" ___

Oh, Ma - ma dear, ___ we're not the for - tu - nate ones. And

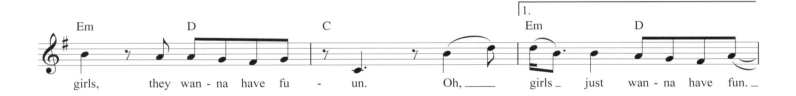

girls, they wan - na have fu - un. Oh, ___ girls ___ just wan - na have fun. ___

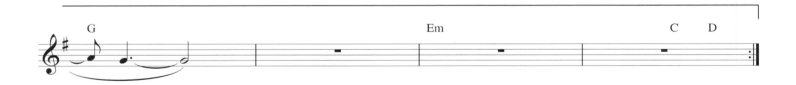

girls just wan - na have... That's all they real - ly want: ___

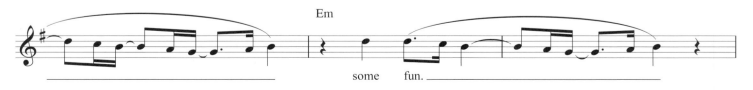

some fun.

When the work - ing day is done, oh, girls, they wan - na have fu -

un. Oh, girls just wan - na have fun.

To Coda ✛

D.C. al Coda
(take 2nd ending)

✛ **Coda**

Outro

They just wan - na, they just wan - na.

They just wan - na, they just wan - na. Girls,

Repeat and fade

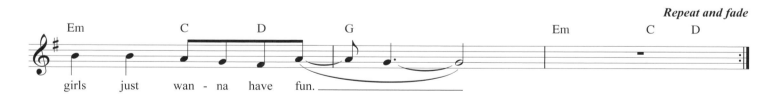

girls just wan - na have fun.

Additional Lyrics

2. The phone rings in the middle of the night.
   My father yells, "What you gonna do with your life?"
   Oh, Daddy dear, you know you're still number one.
   But girls, they wanna have fun.
   Oh, girls just wanna have... *(To Bridge)*

3. Some boys take a beautiful girl
   And hide her away from the rest of the world.
   I wanna be the one to walk in the sun.
   Oh, girls, they wanna have fun.
   Oh, girls just wanna have... *(To Bridge)*

Good Riddance
(Time of Your Life)

Words by Billie Joe
Music by Green Day

Verse
Moderately, in 2

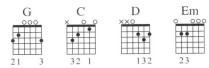

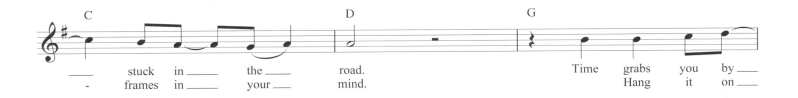

1. An - oth - er turn - ing point, __ a fork __
2. So take the pho - to - graphs __ and still -

__ stuck in __ the __ road. Time grabs you by __
- frames in __ your __ mind. Hang it on __

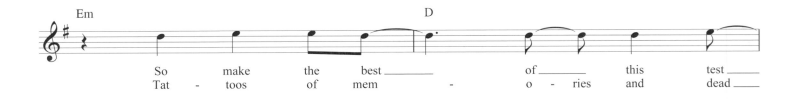

__ the wrist, __ di - rects __ you where __ to __ go.
__ a shelf __ in good __ health and __ good __ time.

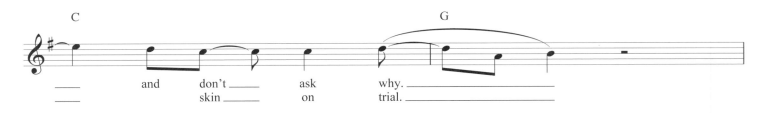

So make the best __ of __ this test __
Tat - toos of mem - o - ries and __ dead __

__ and don't __ ask why. __
__ skin __ on trial. __

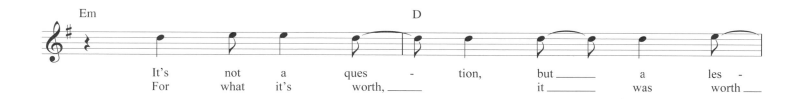

It's not a ques - tion, but _____ a les -
For what it's worth, _____ it _____ was worth _____

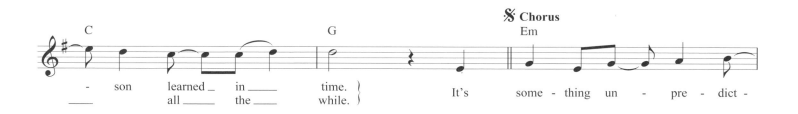

% **Chorus**

- son learned ___ in _____ time.
___ all _____ the _____ while.

It's some - thing un - pre - dict -

- a - ble, ____ but in the end ___ it's right. ____ I

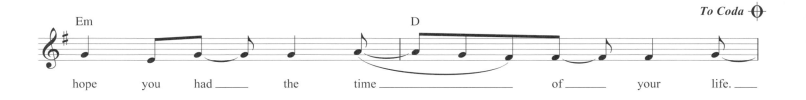

To Coda ⊕

hope you had _____ the time _____ of _____ your life. ____

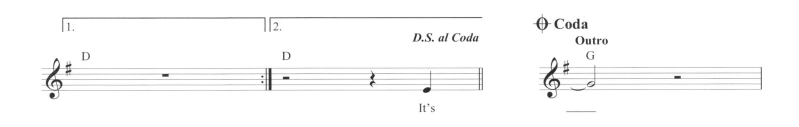

1.   2.   *D.S. al Coda*   ⊕ **Coda**
      Outro

It's

Have a Cigar

Words and Music by Roger Waters

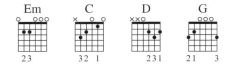

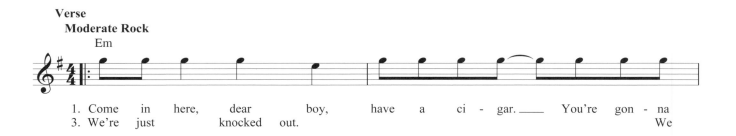

Verse
Moderate Rock

1. Come in here, dear boy, have a ci - gar. ___ You're gon - na
3. We're just knocked out.

go far.
heard a - bout the sell - out.

You're gon - na fly high.
You got - ta get an al - bum out; you

You're
We

nev - er gon - na die. ___ You're gon - na make ___ it if ___ you try. They're ___ gon - na
owe it to ___ the peo - ple. We're so hap - py we can hard - ly count. ___

love you.

2. Well, I've

© 1975 (Renewed) ROGER WATERS OVERSEAS LTD.
All Rights in the U.S. and Canada Administered by WARNER-TAMERLANE PUBLISHING CORP.
All Rights Reserved Used by Permission

Verse

al - ways had a deep re - spect and I mean that most sin - cere - ly.
3. Ev-'ry-bod - y else is just green.   Have ___ you see the chart?

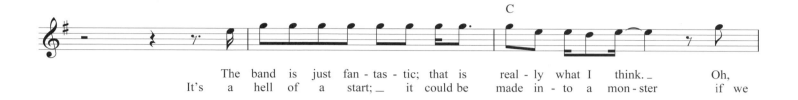

The band is just fan - tas - tic; that is real - ly what I think. _   Oh,
It's a hell of a start; _ it could be made in - to a mon - ster   if we

by the way,   which one's Pink?
all   pull to - geth - er as a team.

Chorus

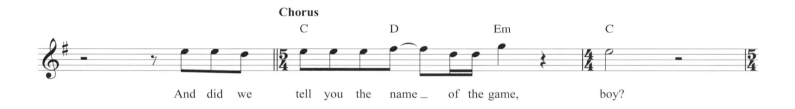

And did we   tell you the name _ of the game,   boy?

We call it "Rid - ing the Gra - vy Train." _____

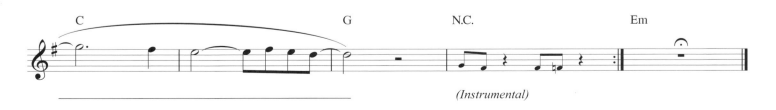

(Instrumental)

Have You Ever Seen the Rain?

Words and Music by John Fogerty

Hey, Soul Sister

Words and Music by Pat Monahan, Espen Lind and Amund Bjorkland

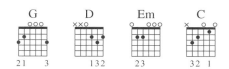

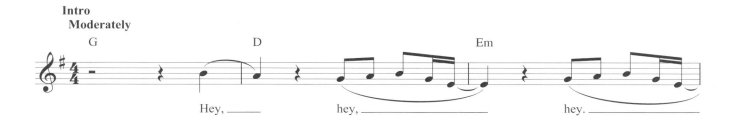

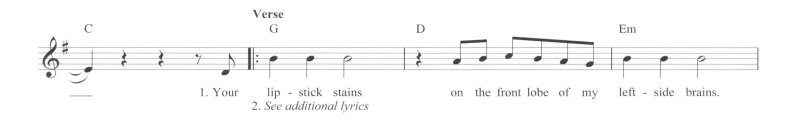

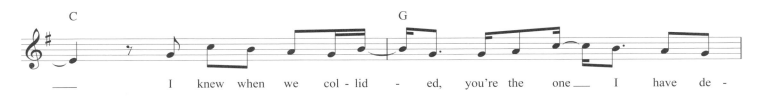

D   Em   C   D

cid - ed   who's one of my   kind.

% Chorus

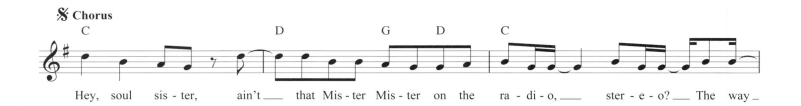

C   D   G   D   C

Hey, soul sis - ter,   ain't   that Mis - ter Mis - ter on the   ra - di - o,   ster - e - o?   The way

To Coda ✛

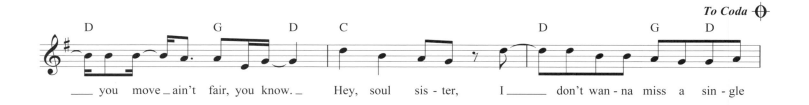

D   G   D   C   D   G   D

  you move ain't fair, you know.   Hey, soul sis - ter, I   don't wan - na miss a sin - gle

1.

C   D   G   D

thing you do   to - night.   Hey,   hey,

2.

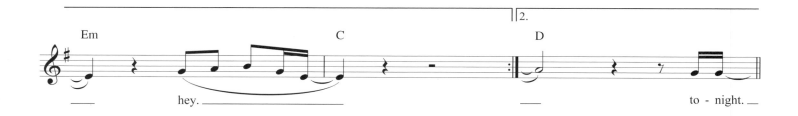

Em   C   D

  hey.   to - night.

Bridge

G   D

  The way you can cut a rug,   watch - ing you's   the on - ly drug   I need.

Em   C

  Some gang - sta, I'm   so thug. You're the   on - ly one   I'm dream - in' of.   You see,

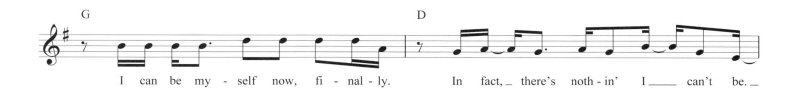

I can be my-self now, fi - nal-ly. In fact, there's noth-in' I can't be.

D.S. al Coda

I want the world to see you'll be with me.

Coda

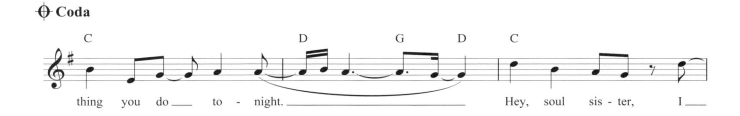

thing you do to - night. Hey, soul sis - ter, I

don't wan-na miss a sin - gle thing you do to - night.

Outro

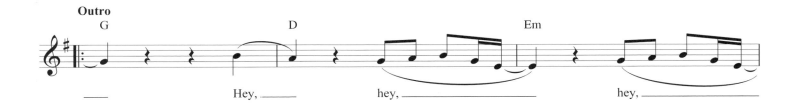

Hey, hey, hey,

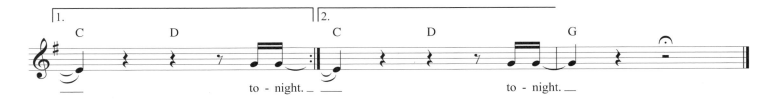

1. to - night. 2. to - night.

Additional Lyrics

2. Just in time, I'm so glad you have a one-track mind like me.
   You gave my life direction,
   A game-show love connection we can't deny.
   I'm so obsessed, my heart is bound to beat right out my un-trimmed chest.
   I believe in you. Like a virgin, you're Madonna
   And I'm always gonna wanna blow your mind.

Home

Words and Music by Jade Castrinos and Alex Ebert

40

Hush-a-bye

Words by Mort Shuman
Music by Doc Pomus

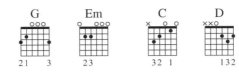

Chorus
Moderately fast

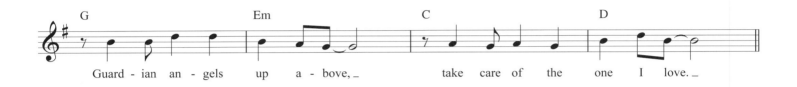

Hush - a - bye, __ hush - a - bye; __ oh, my dar - ling, don't you cry. __

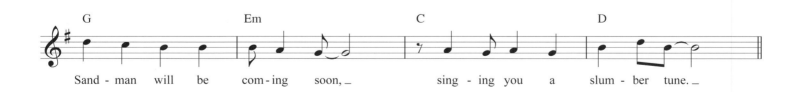

Guard - ian an - gels up a - bove, __ take care of the one I love. __

Interlude

Ooh, _____ ooh. _____

Verse

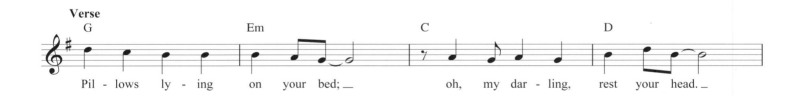

Pil - lows ly - ing on your bed; __ oh, my dar - ling, rest your head. __

Sand - man will be com - ing soon, __ sing - ing you a slum - ber tune. __

Interlude

Ooh, _____ ooh. _____

Ooh. ___ Lull - a -

Bridge

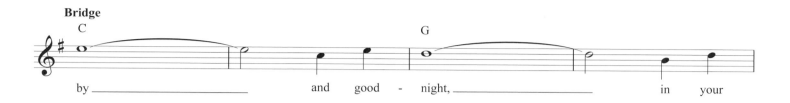

by ___ and good - night, ___ in your

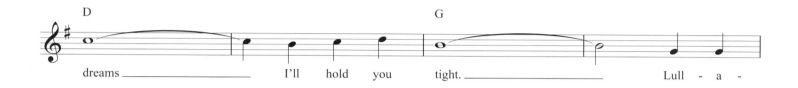

dreams ___ I'll hold you tight. ___ Lull - a -

by ___ and good - night, ___ till the

dawn's ___ ear - ly light. ___

Chorus

Hush - a - bye, ___ hush - a - bye; ___ oh, my dar - ling, don't you cry. ___

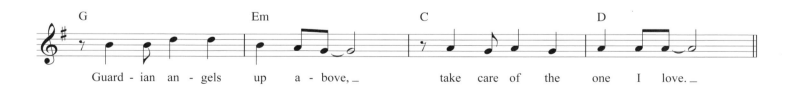

Guard - ian an - gels up a - bove, ___ take care of the one I love. ___

Outro *Repeat and fade*

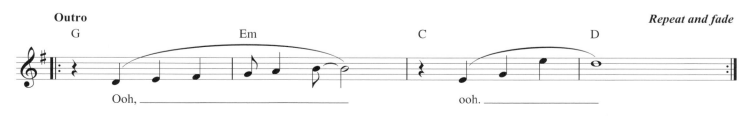

Ooh, ___ ooh. ___

I Knew You Were Trouble.

Words and Music by Taylor Swift, Shellback and Max Martin

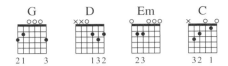

Verse
Moderately, in 2

1. Once up-on a time, a few mis-takes a-go,
2. No a-pol-o-gies, he'll nev-er see you cry. Pre-

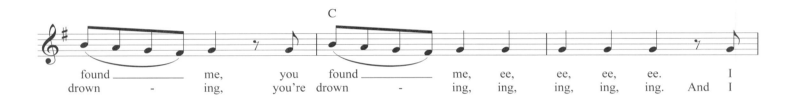

I was in your sights, you got me a-lone. You found ___ me, you
tends he does-n't know that he's the rea-son why you're drown ___ ing, you're

found ___ me, you found ___ me, ee, ee, ee, ee. I
drown ___ ing, you're drown ___ ing, ing, ing, ing, ing. And I

guess you did-n't care, and I guess I liked that. And when I fell hard, you
heard you moved ___ on, from whis-pers on the street. A new notch in your belt is

took a step back with-out ___ me, with-out ___ me, with-
all I'll ev-er be. And now ___ I see, now ___ I see,

Pre-Chorus

out ___ me, ee, ee, ee, ee. And he's long ___
now ___ I see, ee, ee, ee, ee. ___ He was long ___

gone when he's next ___ to ___
gone when he met ___

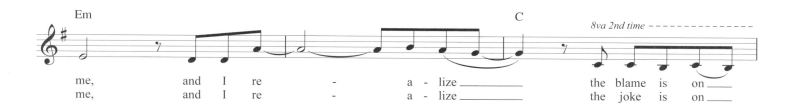

me, and I re - a - lize ___ the blame is on ___
me, and I re - a - lize ___ the joke is on ___

𝄋 **Chorus**

me. ___
me. ___ 'Cause I knew you were trou - ble when you walked in, ___

___ so shame on me now. ___ Flew me to

plac - es I'd nev - er been ___ till you put me down. Oh,

I knew you were trou - ble when you walked in, ___ so

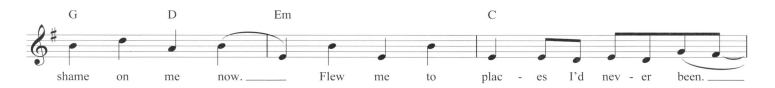

shame on me now. ___ Flew me to plac - es I'd nev - er been. ___

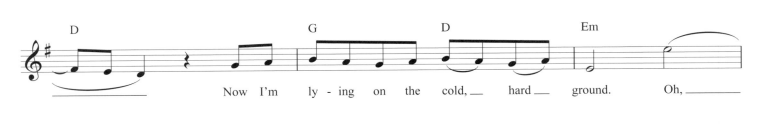

Now I'm ly - ing on the cold, hard ground. Oh,

oh, trou - ble, trou - ble, trou - ble.

To Coda ⊕

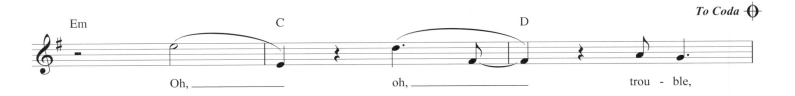

Oh, oh, trou - ble,

1. trou - ble, trou - ble. 2. trou - ble, trou - ble. And the sad - dest fear comes

Bridge

creep - ing in, that you nev - er loved me or her, or

D.S. al Coda   ⊕ **Coda**

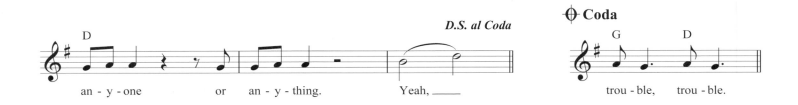

an - y - one or an - y - thing. Yeah, trou - ble, trou - ble.

Outro

I knew you were trou - ble when you walked in. Trou - ble, trou - ble, trou - ble.

I knew you were trou - ble when you walked in. Trou - ble, trou - ble, trou - ble.

46

How to Save a Life

Words and Music by Joseph King and Isaac Slade

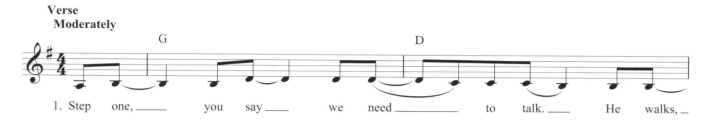

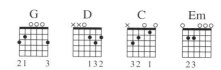

Verse
Moderately

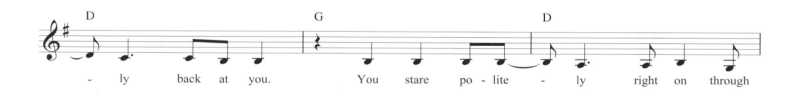

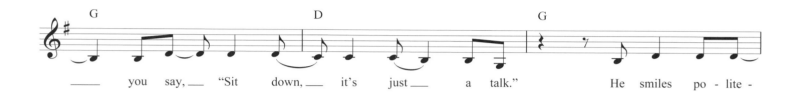

Chorus

Where did I _____ go wrong? _____ I lost _____ a friend
where did I _____ go wrong? _____

some - where _ a - long _____ in the bit - ter - ness. And I would have _ stayed _ up _

_____ with you _ all night had I _ known how to save _____ a life. _

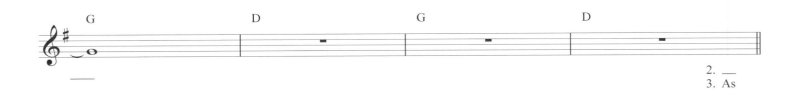

_____ 2. _
3. As

Verse

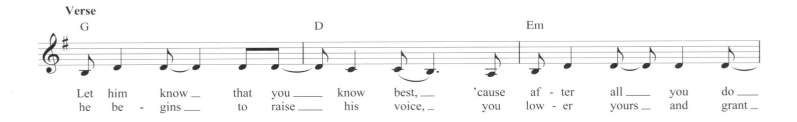

Let him know _ that you _____ know best, _ 'cause af - ter all _____ you do _____
he be - gins _ to raise _____ his voice, _ you low - er yours _ and grant _

_____ know best. _____ Try to slip past his _____ de - fense _
_____ him one _ last choice. _ Drive un - til you lose _____ the road _ or

with - out grant - ing in - no - cence. _____ Lay down _ a list _
break with the ones you've fol - lowed. _____ He will _ do one _

48

_____ of what _ is wrong, the things you've told _____ him all _____ a - long. And
_____ of two _ things: _____ He will ad - mit to ev - 'ry - thing, _____

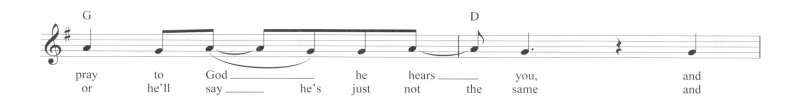

pray to God _____ he hears _____ you, and
or he'll say _____ he's just not the same and

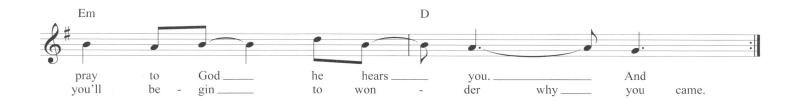

pray to God _____ he hears _____ you. _____ And
you'll be - gin _____ to won - der why _____ you came.

Chorus

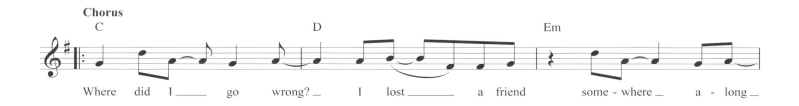

Where did I _____ go wrong? _ I lost _____ a friend some - where _ a - long _

_____ in the bit - ter - ness. And I would have _ stayed _ up _____ with you _ all night

1.

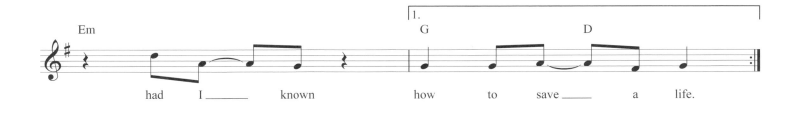

had I _____ known how to save _____ a life.

2.

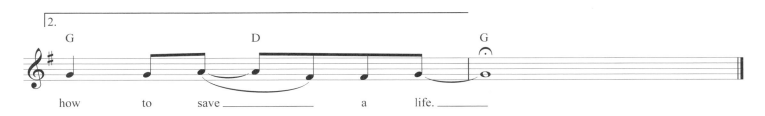

how to save _____ a life. _____

I'll Be

Words and Music by Edwin McCain

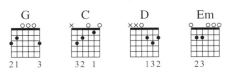

Gently **Verse**

1. The strands in your eyes ___ that col - or them ___ won - der - ful ___
(2.) rain falls ___ an - gry on the tin roof as ___

stop me ___ and steal my ___ breath. ___ And
we lie ___ a - wake in my bed. ___ And

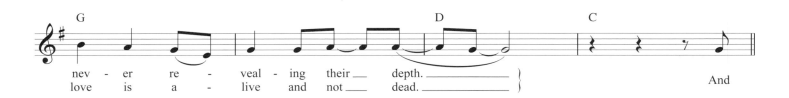

em - 'ralds from moun - tains thrust toward the sky, ___
you're my sur - viv - al, you're my liv - ing proof ___ my

nev - er re - veal - ing their ___ depth. ___ And
love is a - live and not ___ dead. ___ And

Pre-Chorus

tell ___ me that we be - long ___ to - geth - er. ___

Dress it up with the trap - pings of ___ love. ___ I'll

be ___ cap - ti - vat - ed, I'll hang ___ from your ___ lips in -

stead of the gal - lows of heart - ache ___ that hang from a - bove. ___

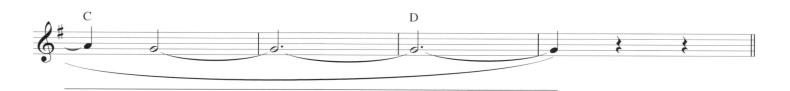

𝄋 Chorus

I'll   be   your   cry - in'   shoul - der. ___

I'll ___ be ___ love su - i - cide. ___ And

I'll   be   bet - ter when I'm old - er. ___

To Coda ⊕

I'll ___ be ___ the great - est fan of your ___

1.

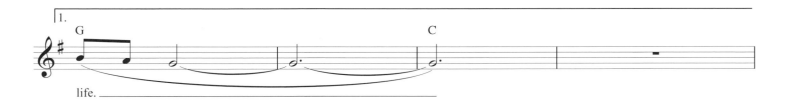

life. ___

2. And

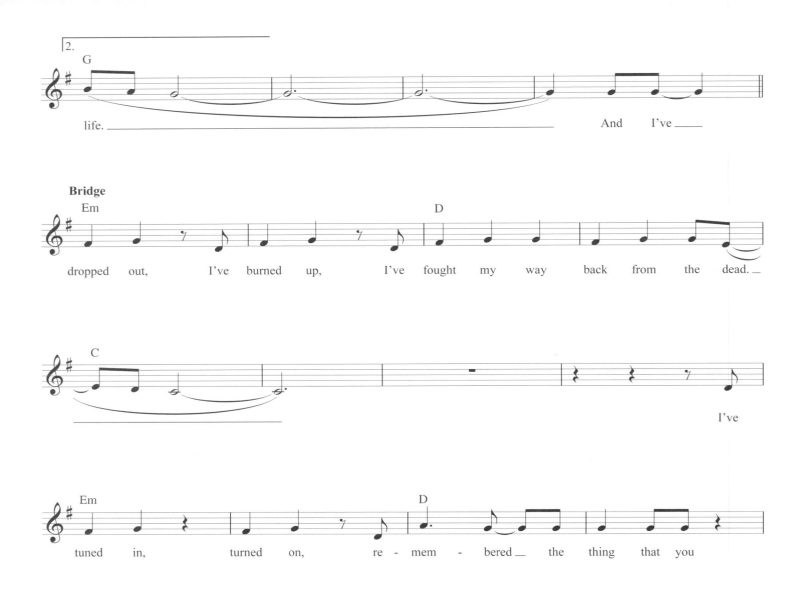

life. _____ And I've _____

Bridge

dropped out, I've burned up, I've fought my way back from the dead. _____

I've

tuned in, turned on, re - mem - bered _____ the thing that you

D.S. al Coda

said. _____

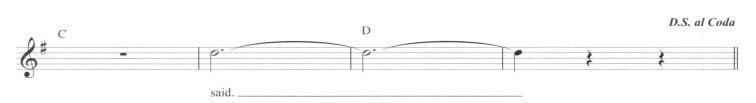

✦ Coda
Outro

life, _____

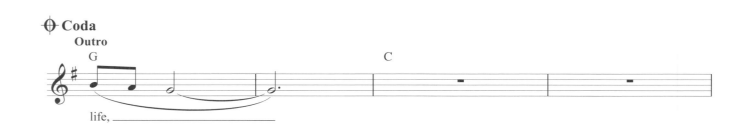

the great - est _____ fan of your _____ life.

If I Had a Hammer
(The Hammer Song)

Words and Music by Lee Hays and Pete Seeger

Additional Lyrics

2. If I had a bell, I'd ring it in the morning,
   I'd ring it in the evening all over this land.
   I'd ring out danger, I'd ring out a warning,
   I'd ring out love between my brothers and my sisters,
   All over this land.

3. If I had a song, I'd sing it in the morning,
   I'd sing it in the evening all over this land.
   I'd sing out danger, I'd sing out a warning,
   I'd sing out love between my brothers and my sisters,
   All over this land.

4. Well, I got a hammer, and I've got a bell,
   And I've got a song to sing all over this land.
   It's the hammer of justice, it's the bell of freedom,
   It's the song about love between my brothers and my sisters,
   All over this land.

Last Kiss

Words and Music by Wayne Cochran

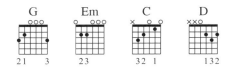

Intro-Chorus
Moderately fast

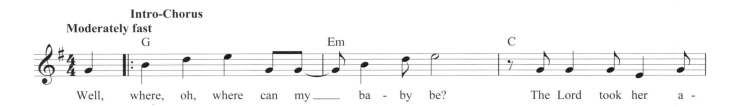

Well, where, oh, where can my ___ ba - by be? The Lord took her a -

way from me. ___ She's gone to heav - en, so I got to be good ___ so

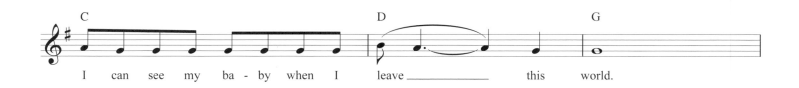

I can see my ba - by when I leave ___ this world.

Verse

1. We were out on a date in my ___ dad - dy's car;
2. Well, when I woke up, the rain was pour - ing down; ___

we had - n't driv - en ver - y far. ___ There in the road ___
there were peo - ple stand - in' all a - round. ___ Some - thing warm ___ a - run - nin'

straight a - head, ___ a car was stalled; the en - gine was dead. ___
in my eyes, ___ but I found ___ my ba - by some - how that night. ___ I

I could-n't stop, __ so I swerved to the right. __ I'll nev-er for-get __ the
raised her head __ and then she smiled and said, __ "Hold me, dar - ling, for a

sound that night: __ the cry - in' tires, __ the bust - in' glass, __ the
lit - tle while." __ I held her close, __ I kissed her our last kiss. __ I

|1.
pain - ful scream __ that I heard last. Well,
found a love __ that I

|2.
knew I would miss. __ But now she's gone; __ e - ven though I hold her tight, I

lost my love, __ my life that night. Well,

Outro-Chorus

where, oh, where can my __ ba - by be? The Lord took her a -

way from me. __ She's gone to heav - en, so I got to be good __ so

I can see my ba - by when I leave __ this world.

Learning to Fly

Words and Music by Tom Petty and Jeff Lynne

Let It Be

Words and Music by John Lennon and Paul McCartney

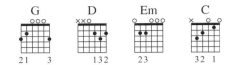

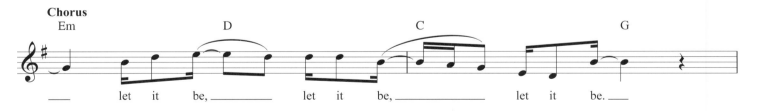

Little Lies

Words and Music by Dave Barnes

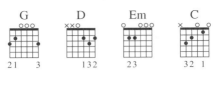

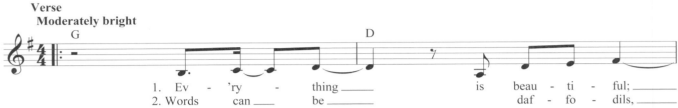

Verse
Moderately bright

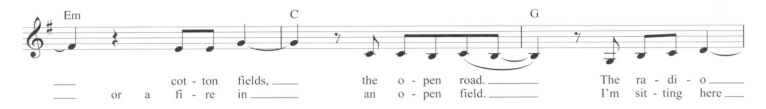

1. Ev - 'ry - thing _____ is beau - ti - ful; _____
2. Words can _____ be _____ daf - fo - dils, _____

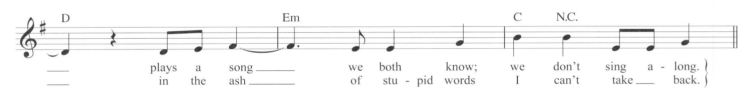

_____ cot - ton fields, _____ the o - pen road. _____ The ra - di - o _____
_____ or a fi - re in _____ an o - pen field. _____ I'm sit - ting here _____

_____ plays a song _____ we both know; we don't sing a - long.
_____ in the ash _____ of stu - pid words I can't take _____ back.

Chorus

La la la la la la la, these lit - tle lies. La la la la la la

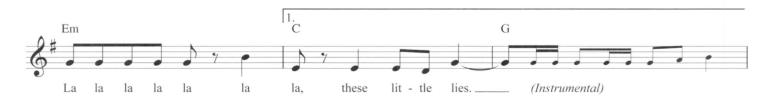

la, these lit - tle lies. _____ La la la la la la la, these lit - tle lies.

1.

La la la la la la la, these lit - tle lies. _____ *(Instrumental)*

Bridge

la, these lit - tle lies. _____ There's a dev - il on my shoul - der, ba -

by, ooh, _____ and I be - lieve _____

_____ too man - y things he says; _____ yeah, _____ yeah, yeah. _____

I'm fight - ing these fears as I find the truth, _____ and I'm

Interlude

sor - ry for hurt - ing you. *(Instrumental)*

Outro-Chorus

La la la la la la la, these lit - tle lies. La la la la la la

la, these lit - tle lies. _____ La la la la la la la, these lit - tle lies.

1.

La la la la la la la, these lit - tle lies.

2.

la, these lit - tle lies.

Lookin' Out My Back Door

Words and Music by John Fogerty

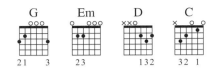

Verse
Moderately, in 2

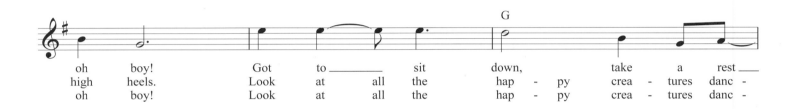

1. Just got home from Il - li - nois, ___ lock the front ___ door,
(2.) gi - ant do - ing cart - wheels, a stat - ue wear - in'
3. For - ward trou - bles Il - li - nois, ___ lock the front ___ door,

oh boy! Got to ___ sit down, take a rest ___
high heels. Look at all the hap - py crea - tures danc -
oh boy! Look at all the hap - py crea - tures danc -

___ on the porch. ___ I - mag - i - na - tion
-ing on the lawn. ___ A di - no - saur ___ Vic -
-ing on the lawn. ___ Both - er me ___ to -

sets in, pret - ty soon ___ I'm sing - in',
tro - la lis - t'ning to ___ Buck O - wens.
mor - row, to - day I'll buy ___ no sor - rows.

Chorus

To Coda ⊕ | 1.

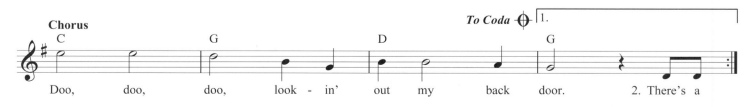

Doo, doo, doo, look - in' out my back door. 2. There's a

door.

Bridge

Tam - bou - rines ____ and el - e - phants are

play - ing in the band. ____ Won't you take a ride ____

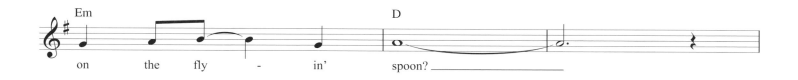

on the fly - in' spoon? ____

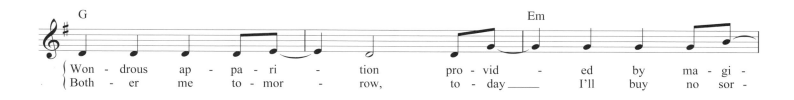

Won - drous ap - pa - ri - tion pro - vid - ed by ma - gi -
Both - er me to - mor - row, to - day ____ I'll buy no sor -

Chorus

- cian.
- rows.

Doo, doo, doo, look - in' out ____

D.C. al Coda   Coda

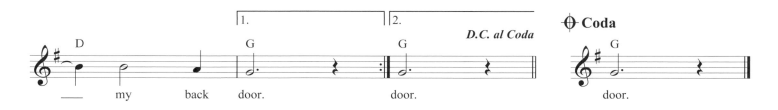

____ my back door.   door.   door.

Love Stinks

Words and Music by Peter Wolf and Seth Justman

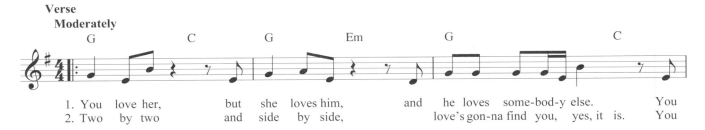

Verse
Moderately

1. You love her, but she loves him, and he loves some-bod-y else. You
2. Two by two and side by side, love's gon-na find you, yes, it is. You

just can't win. And so it goes 'til the day you die. This
just can't hide. You'll feel it call, your heart will fall, then

Pre-Chorus

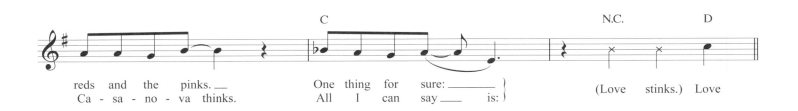

thing they call love, it's gon-na make you cry. I've had the blues, the
love will fly. It's gone; that's all. I don't care what an-y

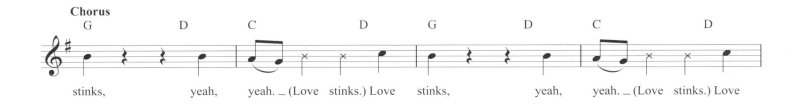

reds and the pinks. One thing for sure: (Love stinks.) Love
Ca-sa-no-va thinks. All I can say is:

Chorus

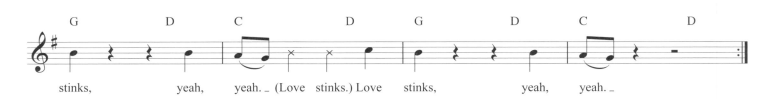

stinks, yeah, yeah. (Love stinks.) Love stinks, yeah, yeah. (Love stinks.) Love

stinks, yeah, yeah. (Love stinks.) Love stinks, yeah, yeah.

Mine

Words and Music by Taylor Swift

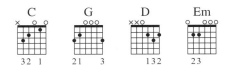

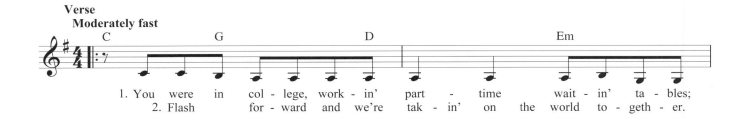

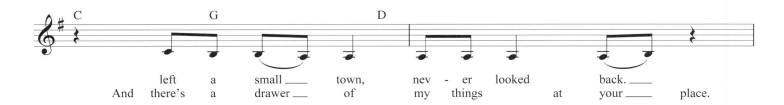

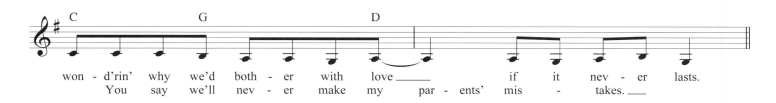

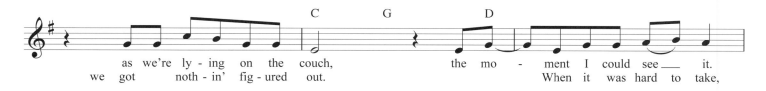

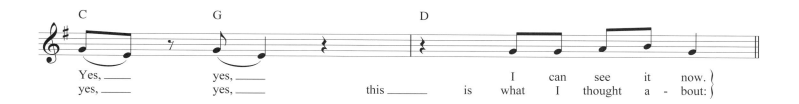

Yes, _____ yes, _____ I can see it now.
yes, _____ yes, _____ this _____ is what I thought a - bout:

Chorus

Do you re - mem - ber? We were sit - tin' there by the wa - ter.

You put your arm a - round me _____ for the first time.

You made a reb - el of a care - less man's care - ful daugh - ter.

1.
You are the best thing that's ev - er been mine. _____

2. **Chorus**

that's ev - er been mine. Do you re - mem - ber all the cit - y lights on the wa - ter?

You saw me start to be - lieve _____ for the first time. You made a reb - el of a

care - less man's care - ful daugh - ter. You are the best thing that's ev - er been mine.

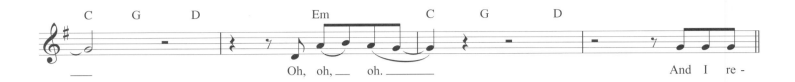

Oh, oh, — oh. — And I re -

Bridge

mem - ber that fight, two - thir - ty A. M., 'cause ev - 'ry - thing was slip - pin' right

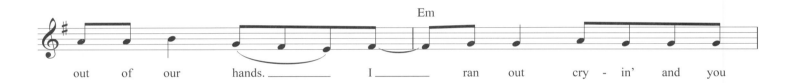

out of our hands. I ran out cry - in' and you

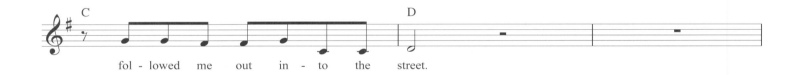

fol - lowed me out in - to the street.

Braced my - self for the good - bye, 'cause that's all

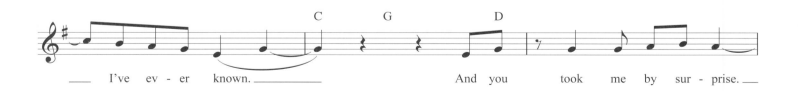

I've ev - er known. And you took me by sur - prise.

You said, "I'll nev - er leave you a - lone."

Chorus

You said, "I re-mem-ber how we felt sit-tin' by the wa-ter.

And ev-'ry time I look at you, ___ it's like the first time. I fell in love with a

care-less man's care-ful daugh-ter. She is the best ___ thing that's ev-er been ___ mine." ___

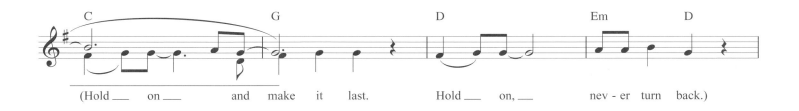

(Hold ___ on ___ and make it last. Hold ___ on, ___ nev-er turn back.)

You made a reb-el of a care-less's man's care-ful daugh-ter.

Outro

You are the best thing that's ev-er been mine. ___ (Hold ___ on.) ___

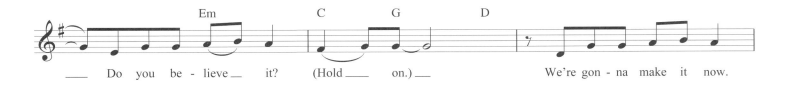

___ Do you be-lieve ___ it? (Hold ___ on.) ___ We're gon-na make it now.

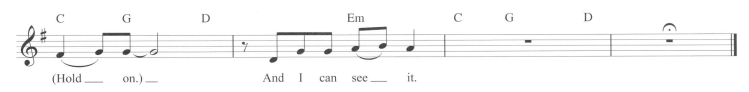

(Hold ___ on.) ___ And I can see ___ it.

On the Turning Away

Words and Music by David Jon Gilmour and Anthony John Moore

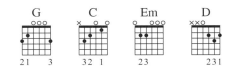

Additional Lyrics

3. On the wings of the night,
   As the daytime is stirring,
   Where the speechless unite in a silent accord,
   Using words you will find are strange,
   Mesmerized as they light the flame.
   Feel the new wind of change on the wings of the night.

4. No more turning away
   From the weak and the weary.
   No more turning away from the coldness inside.
   Just a world that we all must share.
   It's not enough just to stand and stare.
   Is it only a dream that there'll be no more turning away?

Let Her Cry

**Words and Music by Darius Carlos Rucker, Everett Dean Felber,
Mark William Bryan and James George Sonefeld**

Verse
Moderately slow Rock

1. She sits a-lone by a lamp-post

tryin' to find a thought that's es-caped her mind.

She says, "Dad's the one I love the most,

but Stipe's not far be-hind."

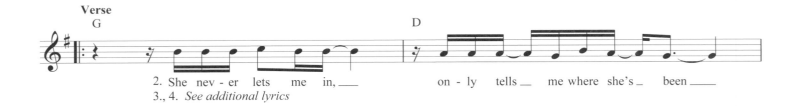

Verse

2. She nev - er lets me in, ___ on - ly tells ___ me where she's ___ been ___
3., 4. *See additional lyrics*

when she's had ___ too much to drink. ___

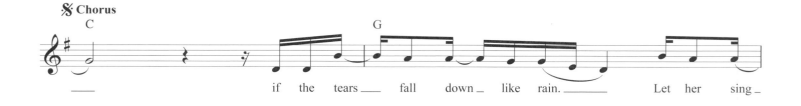

I say that I don't ___ care. ___ I just run my hands through her dark hair, ___ then I

pray to God, ___ "You got - ta help me fly ___ a - way." ___ And just let her cry ___

Chorus

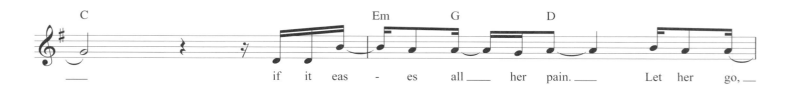

___ if the tears ___ fall down ___ like rain. ___ Let her sing ___

___ if it eas - es all ___ her pain. ___ Let her go, ___

let her walk ___ right out on ___ me. _____ And if the

sun comes up to-mor - row, let her be, ___ { let her be. ___ { oh. ___

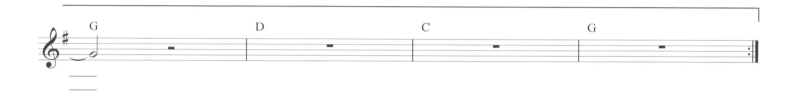

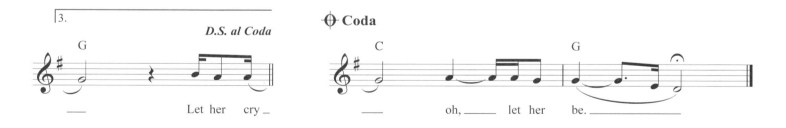

D.S. al Coda

Let her cry ___ ___ oh, ___ let her be. ___

Additional Lyrics

3. This morning I woke up alone,
   Found a note standing by the phone
   Sayin', "Maybe, maybe I'll be back someday."
   I wanted to look for you; you walked in.
   I didn't know just what to do,
   So I sat back down, had a beer and felt sorry for myself.

4. Last night I tried to leave.
   Cried so much, I could not believe
   She was the same girl I fell in love with long ago.
   She went in the back to get high.
   I sat down on my couch and cried,
   Yelling, "Oh, Mama, please help me. Won't you hold my hand?"

One Love

Words and Music by Bob Marley

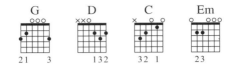

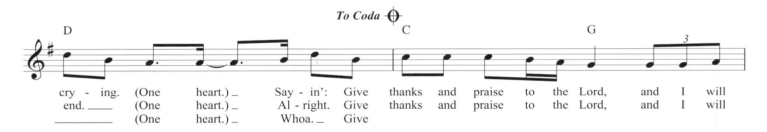

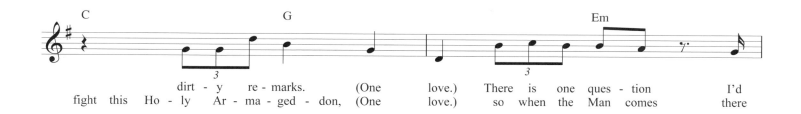

dirty re-marks. (One love.) There is one ques-tion I'd
fight this Ho-ly Ar-ma-ged-don, (One love.) so when the Man comes there

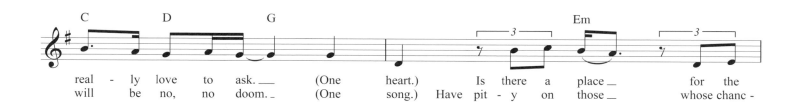

real-ly love to ask. (One heart.) Is there a place for the
will be no, no doom. (One song.) Have pit-y on those whose chanc-

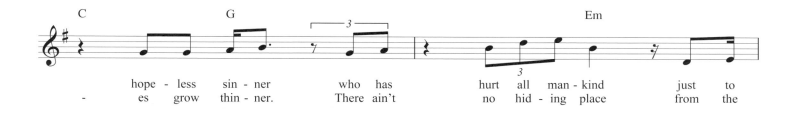

hope-less sin-ner who has hurt all man-kind just to
es grow thin-ner. There ain't no hid-ing place just from the

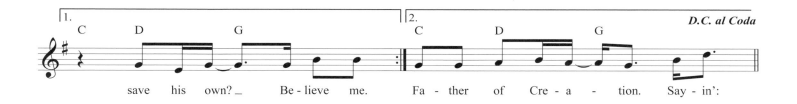

1.
save his own? Be-lieve me.
2. *D.C. al Coda*
Fa-ther of Cre-a-tion. Say-in':

⊕ Coda

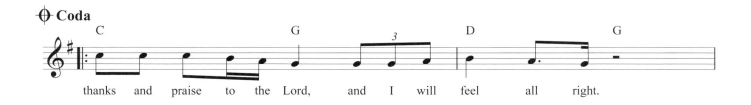

thanks and praise to the Lord, and I will feel all right.

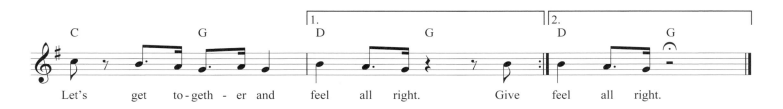

Let's get to-geth-er and feel all right. Give feel all right.

One of Us

Words and Music by Eric Bazilian

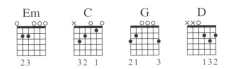

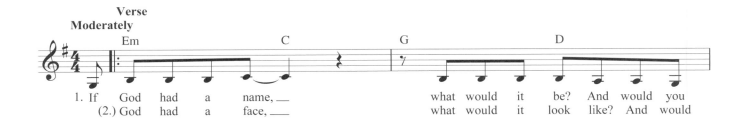

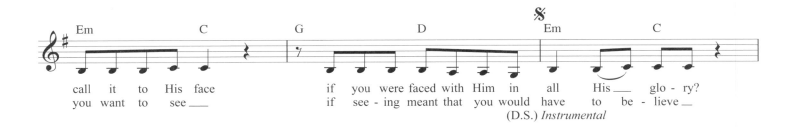

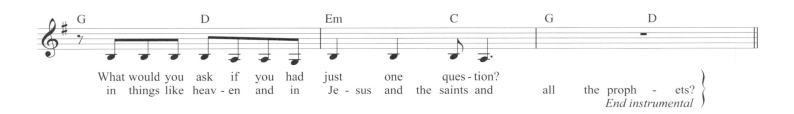

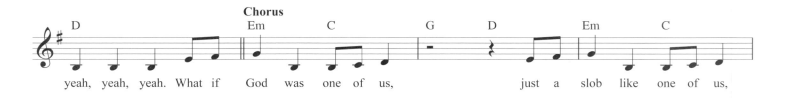

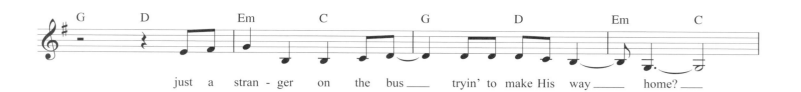

just a stran-ger on the bus ___ tryin' to make His way ___ home? ___

1.

2., 3.

2. If Tryin' to make His way ___ home, ___

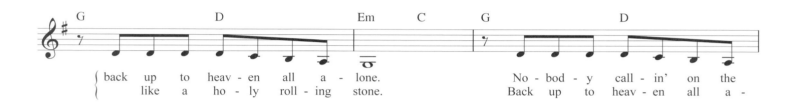

back up to heav-en all a - lone.
like a ho-ly roll-ing stone. No-bod-y call-in' on the
Back up to heav-en all a -

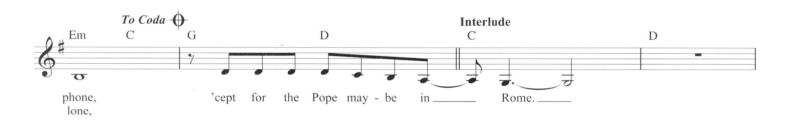

To Coda ⊕

Interlude

phone, 'cept for the Pope may-be in ___ Rome. ___
lone,

D.S. al Coda
(take 2nd ending)

⊕ **Coda**

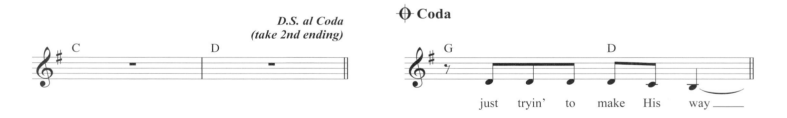

just tryin' to make His way ___

Outro

___ home. ___ No-bod-y call-in' on the

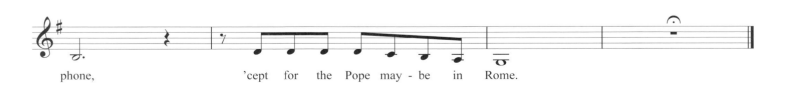

phone, 'cept for the Pope may-be in Rome.

Save Tonight

Words and Music by Eagle Eye Cherry

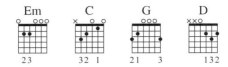

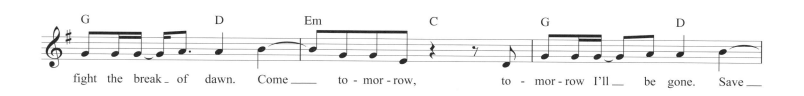

fight the break __ of dawn. Come _____ to - mor - row, to - mor - row I'll __ be gone. Save ___

To Coda ⊕

___ to - night, and fight the break __ of dawn. Come _____ to - mor - row, to -

Bridge

mor - row I'll __ be gone. 2. There's a mor - row I'll __ be gone. To - mor - row comes to

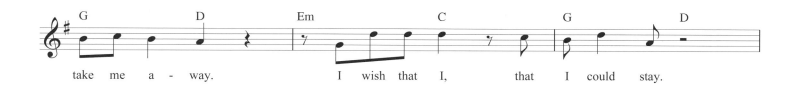

take me a - way. I wish that I, that I could stay.

Girl, you know I've got to go, oh. Lord, I wish it was - n't so.

⊕ **Coda**

D.S. al Coda   **Outro**

Save to - mor - row I'll __ be gone. To -

Play 4 times

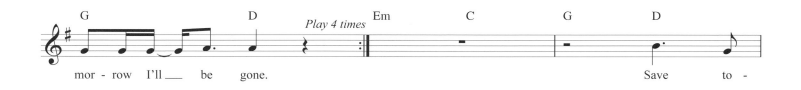

mor - row I'll __ be gone. Save to -

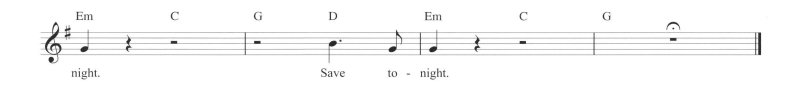

night. Save to - night.

The Scientist

Words and Music by Guy Berryman, Jon Buckland, Will Champion and Chris Martin

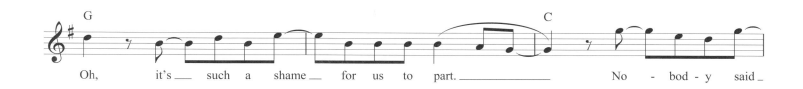

Oh, it's ___ such a shame ___ for us to part. _____ No - bod - y said ___

___ it was eas - y. _____ No ___ one ev - er said ___ it would be { this ___ hard. ___ / so ___ hard. ___

___ { Oh, take me / I'm go - ing } back to the start. _____

Outro

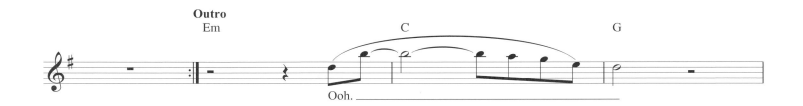

Ooh. _____

Ah, ooh. _____

Ah, ooh. _____

Additional Lyrics

2. I was just guessing at numbers and figures,
   Pulling the puzzles apart.
   Questions of science, science and progress
   Do not speak as loud as my heart.
   And tell me you love me, come back and haunt me.
   Oh, and I rush to the start.
   Running in circles, chasing our tails,
   Coming back as we are.

Slip Slidin' Away

Words and Music by Paul Simon

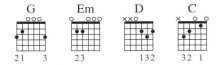

Slip slid - in' a - way. Slip slid - in' a -

way. _____ You know the

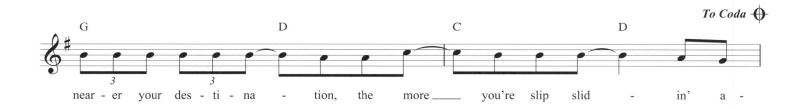

near - er your des - ti - na - tion, the more _____ you're slip slid - in' a -

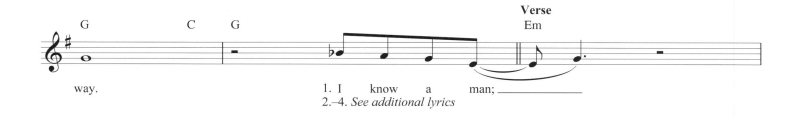

way.

1. I know a man; _____
2.–4. *See additional lyrics*

he came from my home - town. _____ He wore his

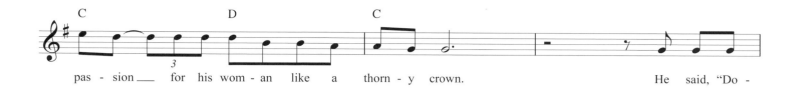

pas - sion___ for his wom - an like a thorn - y crown. He said, "Do -

lor - es,_____ I_____ live in fear._____

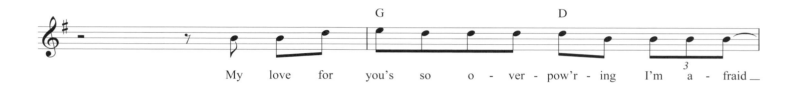

My love for you's so o - ver - pow'r - ing I'm a - fraid___

___ that I_____ will dis - ap - pear." Slip slid - in' a -

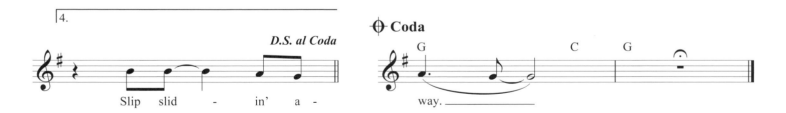

Slip slid - in' a - way._____

Additional Lyrics

2. And I know a woman; became a wife.
   These are the very words she uses to describe her life.
   She said, "A good day ain't got no rain."
   She said, "A bad day's when I lie in bed and think of things that might have been."

3. And I know a father who had a son.
   He longed to tell him all the reasons for the things he'd done.
   He came a long way just to explain.
   He kissed his boy as he lay sleeping, then he turned around and headed home again.

4. God only knows. God makes His plan.
   The information's unavailable to the mortal man.
   We're workin' our jobs, collect our pay,
   Believe we're glidin' down the highway, when in fact, we're slip slidin' away.

Stand by Me

Words and Music by Jerry Leiber, Mike Stoller and Ben E. King

Chorus

stand _____ by me, _____ oh, _____ stand _____ by _____

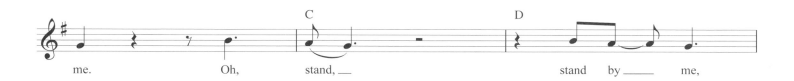

me. Oh, stand, ___ stand by _____ me,

stand by _____ me. 2. If the sky _ Dar - lin', dar - lin',

Outro-Chorus

stand _____ by me, _____ oh, _____ stand _____

___ by _____ me. Oh, stand, ___

stand by _____ me, stand by _____ me.

Additional Lyrics

2. If the sky that we look upon should tumble and fall,
   Or the mountains should crumble to the sea,
   I won't cry, I won't cry. No, I won't shed a tear,
   Just as long as you stand, stand by me.
   And darlin', darlin'… (*To Chorus*)

The Story

Words and Music by Phil Hanseroth

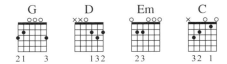

Additional Lyrics

2. I climbed across the mountaintops,
Swam all across the ocean blue.
I crossed all the lines and I broke all the rules,
But, baby, I broke them all for you.
Oh, because even when I was flat broke,
You made me feel like a million bucks. You do.
I was made for you.

3. You see the smile that's on my mouth?
It's hiding the words that don't come out.
All of my friends who think that I'm blessed,
They don't know my head is a mess.
No, they don't know who I really am,
And they don't know what I've been through like you do.
And I was made for you.

Push

Written by Rob Thomas with Matt Serletic

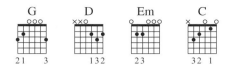

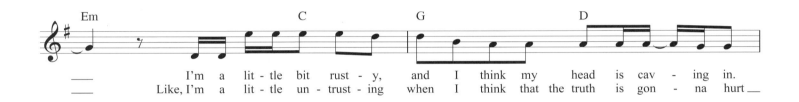

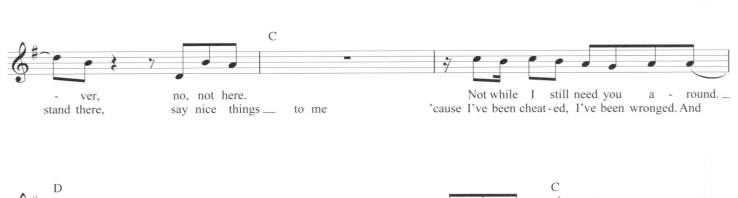

-ver,   no, not here.   Not while I still need you a - round. __
stand there,   say nice things __ to me   'cause I've been cheat-ed, I've been wronged. And

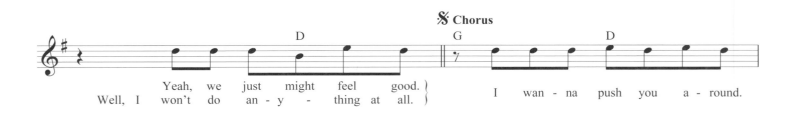

__   You don't owe __ me.   We might change, __ yeah.
you,   you don't know __ me.   Yeah, well, I   can't change.

% Chorus

      Yeah, we just might feel good. }   I wan - na push you a - round.
Well, I won't do an-y-thing at all. }

Well, I will, well, I will.   I wan - na push you __ down.   Well, I will,   well, I will.

To Coda ⊕

I wan - na take you for grant - ed.   I wan - na take you for grant -

ed, yeah, yeah, I will and I will, _____   and I __

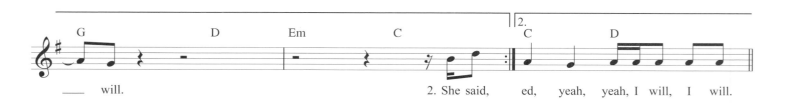

__ will.   2. She said, ed, yeah, yeah, I will, I will.

Bridge

Oh, but don't bowl me o - ver. Just wait a min - ute, well, it kind - a fell a -

part. Things get so cra - zy, cra - zy. Don't rush this, ba -

D.S. al Coda

- by. Don't rush this, ba - by, ba - by.

Coda

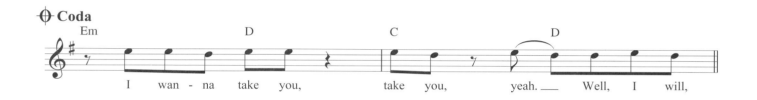

I wan - na take you, take you, yeah. Well, I will,

Outro

and I will, I will, I will, yeah. And I will, I will,

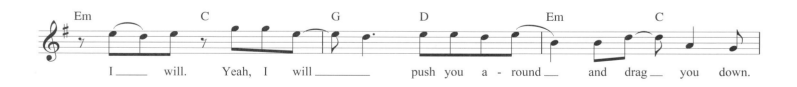

I will. Yeah, I will push you a - round and drag you down.

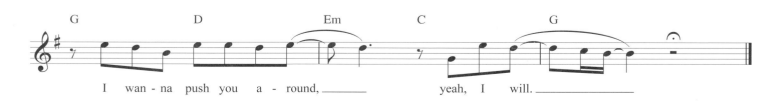

I wan - na push you a - round, yeah, I will.

The Swimming Song

Words and Music by Loudon Wainwright III

Additional Lyrics

2. This summer I did the backstroke, and you know that that's not all.
I did the breaststroke and the butterfly and the old Australian crawl,
The old Australian crawl.
This summer I swam in a public place and a reservoir to boot.
At the latter I was informal, at the former I wore my suit,
I wore my swimming suit.

3. This summer I did swan dives and jackknives for you all.
But once, when you weren't looking, I did a cannonball,
Did a cannonball.
This summer I went swimming. This summer I might have drowned.
But I held my breath and I kicked my feet and I moved my arms around,
Moved my arms around.

A Teenager in Love

Words by Doc Pomus
Music by Mort Shuman

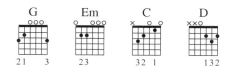

Additional Lyrics

2. One day I feel so happy, next day I feel so sad.
   I guess I'll learn to take the good with the bad.

3. If you want to make me cry, that won't be so hard to do.
   And if you should say goodbye, I'll still go on loving you.

This One's for the Girls

Words and Music by Aimee Mayo, Hillary Lindsey and Chris Lindsey

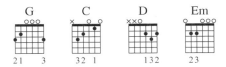

Verse
Moderately

1. This is for all ___ you girls ___ a-bout ___ thir-teen. ___
2., 3. *See additional lyrics*

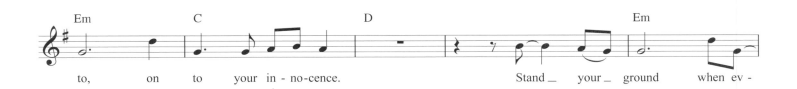

High school can be ___ so rough, ___ can be ___ so mean. ___ Hold ___ on ___

to, on to your in-no-cence. Stand ___ your ___ ground when ev-

- 'ry-bod-y's giv-in' in. This ___ one's for the girls. ___ one's for the girls ___

Chorus

who've ev- ___ er had a bro-ken heart, ___ who've wished ___

up-on a shoot-ing star. ____ You're beau - ti - ful the way you are. ____ This __

____ one's for the girls ____ who love ____ with-out hold-ing back, ____ who dream __

To Coda ⊕

____ with ev -'ry-thing they have, __ all a - round __ the world. This __

D.C. al Coda
(take 2nd ending)

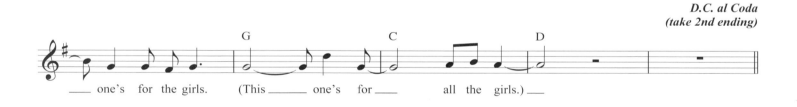

____ one's for the girls. (This ____ one's for ____ all the girls.) ____

⊕ **Coda**

Bridge

____ one's for the girls. Yeah, __ we're all __ the same __ in - side _ (the same __

____ in - side), _ from one __ to nine-ty - nine. ____ This __ one's for the girls __

Chorus

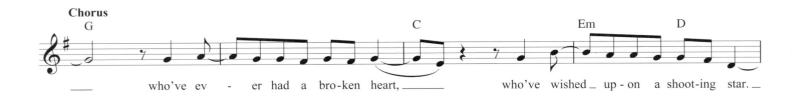

_____ who've ev - er had a bro-ken heart, _____ who've wished _ up - on a shoot-ing star. _

_____ You're beau - ti - ful the way you are. _____ This _ one's for the girls _

_____ who love _ with-out hold-ing back, _____ who dream _ with ev -'ry-thing they have, _

_____ all a - round _ the world. This _ one's for the girls.

Outro

(This _____ one's for _____ all the girls.) _ Yeah, this _ one's for the girls.

(This _____ one's for _____ all the girls.) _

Additional Lyrics

2. This is for all you girls about twenty-five
   In little apartments, just tryin' to get by,
   Livin' on, on dreams and Spaghetti-O's,
   Wonderin' where your life's gonna go.

3. This is for all you girls about forty-two,
   Tossin' pennies in the fountain of youth.
   Every laugh, laugh line on your face
   Made you who you are today.

Today Was a Fairytale

Words and Music by Taylor Swift

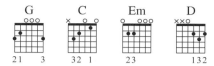

1. To - day was a fair - y - tale. You were the prince. I used to be a
3. *See additional lyrics*

dam - sel in dis - tress. You took me by the hand and you picked me up at

six. To - day was a fair - y - tale.

2. To - day was a fair - y - tale. I wore a
4. *See additional lyrics*

dress, you wore a dark grey T - shirt. You told me I was

pret - ty when I looked like a mess. To - day was a fair - y - tale.

Pre-Chorus

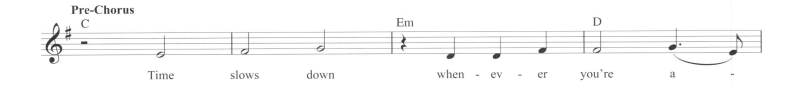

Time slows down when - ev - er you're a -

round. _____ But can you

%. Chorus

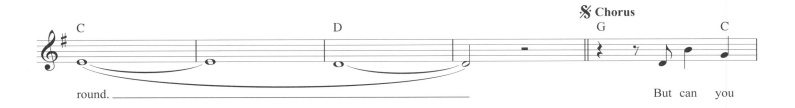

feel this mag - ic in the air? It must have been the way you kissed me. _____ Fell in

To Coda ⊕

love when I saw you stand - in' there. It must -'ve been the way to - day was a

fair - y - tale. _____ It must -'ve been the way to - day was a

fair - y - tale. _____

Bridge

Time

slows   down   when - ev - er   you're   a - round.   I   can

feel   my   heart;   it's   beat - ing   in ____ my   chest. ____   Did   you

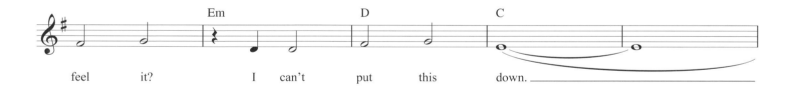

feel   it?   I   can't   put   this   down. _____

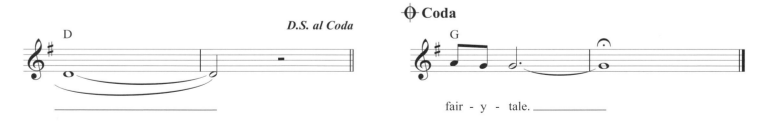

D.S. al Coda

✛ Coda

_____

fair - y - tale. _____

Additional Lyrics

3. Today was a fairytale.
   You've got a smile
   Takes me to another planet.
   Every move you make,
   Everything you say is right.
   Today was a fairytale.

4. Today was a fairytale.
   All that I can say
   Is now it's getting so much clearer.
   Nothing made sense
   Till the time I saw your face.
   Today was a fairytale.

3 AM

Lyrics by Rob Thomas
Music by Rob Thomas, Brian Yale, John Leslie Goff and John Joseph Stanley

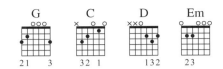

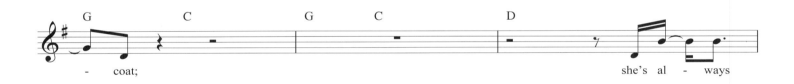

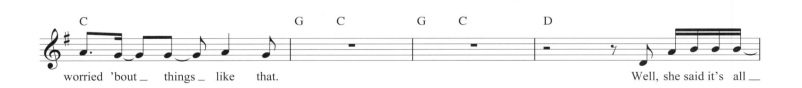

Pre-Chorus

And she on - ly sleeps _ when it's rain - ing, and she screams _

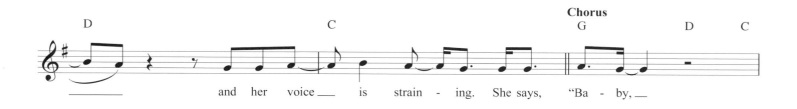

Chorus

_ and her voice _ is strain - ing. She says, "Ba - by, _

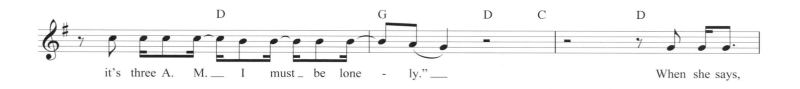

it's three A. M. _ I must _ be lone - ly." _ When she says,

"Ba - by," _ well, I can't help _ but be scared _ of it all _

1.

_ some - times. And the rain's gon - na wash a - way; _ I be - lieve it.

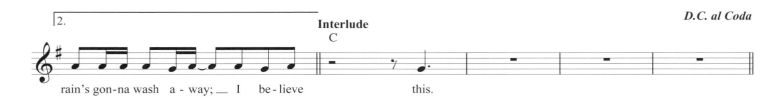

2. *D.C. al Coda*

Interlude

rain's gon-na wash a - way; _ I be - lieve this.

Coda

But out-side it's stopped rain-ing, _____ yeah. But she _ says,

Outro-Chorus

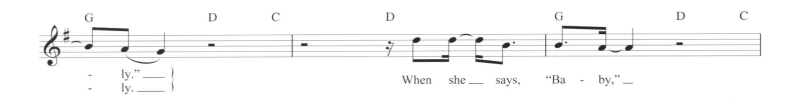

"Ba - by, _____
_____ this. _____

well, it's three A. M. ___ I must _ be lone -
Well, it's three A. M. ___ I must _ be lone -

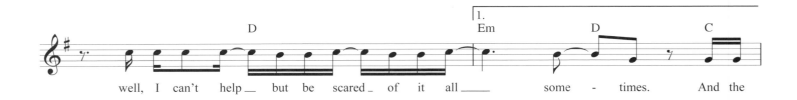

- ly." ___
- ly. ___

When she ___ says, "Ba - by," _

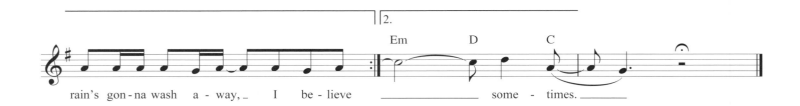

1.

well, I can't help _ but be scared _ of it all ____ some - times. And the

2.

rain's gon-na wash a - way, _ I be - lieve _____ some - times. _____

Additional Lyrics

2. Well, she's got a little bit of something;
   God, it's better than nothing.
   And in her color portrait world,
   She believes that she's got it all.
   She swears the moon don't hang
   Quite as high as it used to.

3. Well, she believes that life isn't made up
   Of all that she's used to.
   And the clock on the wall has been stuck
   At three for days and days.
   She thinks that happiness
   Is a mat that sits on her doorway.

With or Without You

Words and Music by U2

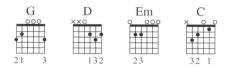

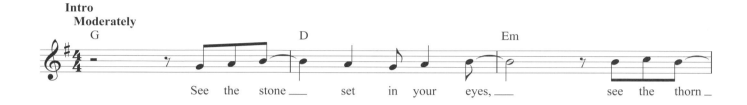

See the stone ___ set in your eyes, ___ see the thorn ___

___ twist in your side. ___ I'll wait ___ for you.

1. Sleight of hand ___ and twist of fate, ___ on a bed of nails ___
2. Through the storm ___ we reach the shore. ___ You give it all, ___

___ she makes me wait, ___ and I wait ___ with - out ___ you, ___
___ but I want more, ___ and I'm wait - ing for ___ you, ___

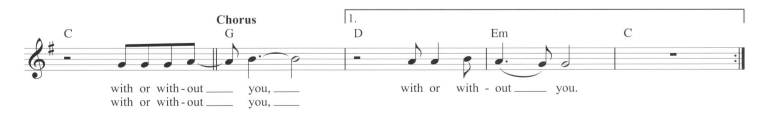

with or with-out ___ you, ___ with or with - out ___ you.
with or with-out ___ you, ___

with or with-out you,___ uh - huh.___ I can't live___

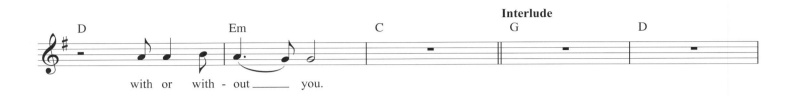
Interlude
with or with-out ___ you.

% Bridge
And you give your-self a - way.___ And you give___

___ your-self a - way.___ And you give,___ and you give,___

To Coda ⊕
___ and you give your-self a - way.___

Verse
3. My hands are tied,___ my bod-y bruised.___

___ You got ___ me with ___ noth-ing to win ___ and ___

nothing left to lose. And you

Coda

With or without

Chorus

you, with or without you, oh. I can't live

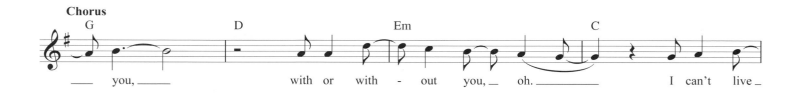

with or without you. Oh.

Interlude

Oh. Oh, oh, oh.

Outro-Chorus

With or without you, with or with-

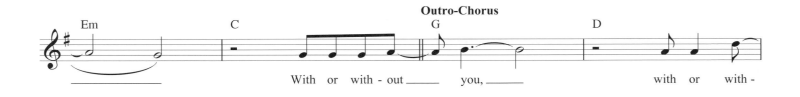

out you, uh-huh. I can't live with or with-

out you, with or without you.

Two Princes

Words and Music by Spin Doctors

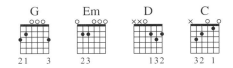

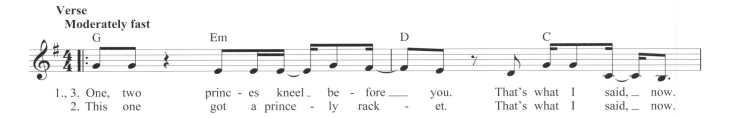

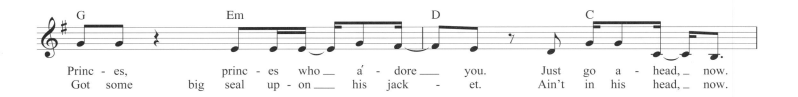

1., 3. One, two princ-es kneel be-fore you. That's what I said, now.
2. This one got a prince-ly rack-et. That's what I said, now.

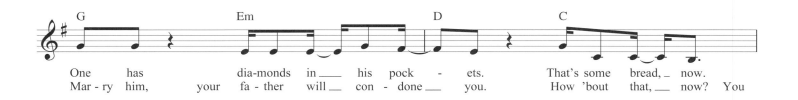

Princ-es, princ-es who a'-dore you. Just go a-head, now.
Got some big seal up-on his jack-et. Ain't in his head, now.

One has dia-monds in his pock-ets. That's some bread, now.
Mar-ry him, your fa-ther will con-done you. How 'bout that, now? You

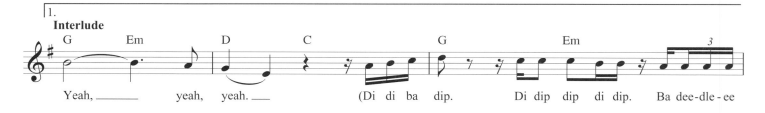

This one, he wants to buy you rock-ets. Ain't in his head, now.
mar-ry me, your fa-ther will dis-own you. He'll eat his hat, now.

1.

Interlude

Yeah, yeah, yeah. (Di di ba dip. Di dip dip di dip. Ba dee-dle-ee

di ba du ba du ba du ba du ba du ba du ba du ba du ba.)

2., 3.

Pre-Chorus

Mar - ry him or mar - ry me. I'm ___ the one that loves you, ba - by. Can't you see? I ain't

got no fu - ture or a fam - 'ly tree, ___ but I know what a prince and lov - er ought to be. ___

Chorus

I know what a prince and lov - er ought to be. ___ Said, if you want to call ___ me, ba -

- by, just go a - head, ___ now. And if you'd like to tell ___ me may -

- be, just go a - head, ___ now. And if you wan - na buy ___ me flow -

To Coda

- ers, just go a - head, ___ now. And if you'd like to talk ___ for ho -

D.C. al Coda
(take 2nd ending)

Coda

- urs, just go a - head, ___ now.

- urs, just go a - head, ___ now.

Wagon Wheel

Words and Music by Ketch Secor and Bob Dylan

see my ba - by to - night. _____ So, rock ___ me, ma - ma, like a

wag - on wheel. _ Rock ___ me, ma - ma, an - y way you feel. _ Hey, _

___ me, ma - ma, like the wind and the rain. _ Rock ___ me, ma - ma, like a

south - bound train. Hey, _____ ma - ma, rock ___ me.

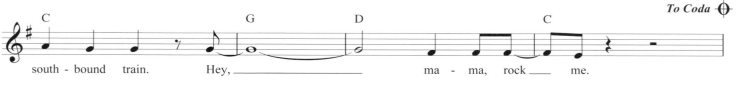

Oh, _____ so rock _

Additional Lyrics

2. Runnin' from the cold up in New England,
   I was born to be a fiddler in an old-time string band.
   My baby plays the guitar, I pick a banjo now.
   Oh, North Country winters keep a-gettin' me down.
   Lost my money playin' poker, so I had to leave town.
   But I ain't turnin' back to livin' that old life no more.

3. Walkin' through the South out of Roanoke,
   I caught a trucker out of Philly, had a nice long toke.
   But he's a-headin' west from the Cumberland Gap to Johnson City, Tennessee.
   I got, I gotta move on before the sun.
   I hear my baby callin' my name and I know that she's the only one.
   And if I die in Raleigh, at least I will die free.

Wonderful Tonight

Words and Music by Eric Clapton

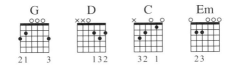

Verse
Moderately

1. It's late in the eve - ning; she's won-d'ring what clothes __
2. We go to a par - ty, ev - 'ry - one turns __
3. It's time to go home __ now, I've got an ach -

__ to wear. __ She puts on her make - up
__ to see __ this beau - ti - ful la - dy
- ing head. __ So I give her the car __ keys,

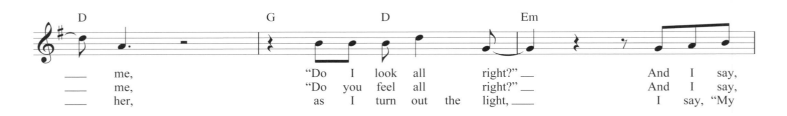

and brush - es her long, __ blonde hair. __ And then she asks __
is walk - ing a - round __ with me. __ And then she asks __
and she helps me to bed. __ And then I tell __

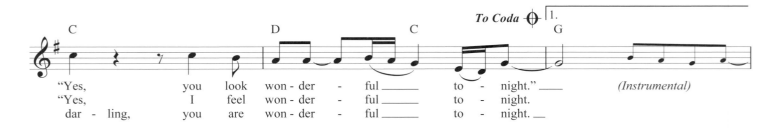

__ me, "Do I look all right?" __ And I say,
__ me, "Do you feel all right?" __ And I say,
__ her, as I turn out the light, __ I say, "My

To Coda ⊕ | 1.

"Yes, you look won - der - ful __ to - night." __ *(Instrumental)*
"Yes, I feel won - der - ful __ to - night.
dar - ling, you are won - der - ful __ to - night. __

Bridge

I feel won - der - ful ___ be - cause I see ___ the love ___

___ light in ___ your eyes. Then the won-der of it all ___ is that you

just don't re - al - ize ___ how much ___ I love ___ you." *(Instrumental)*

D.C. al Coda

Coda

Outro

Oh, my dar - ling, you are won - der - ful ___ to - night." _

___ *(Instrumental)*

Zombie

Lyrics and Music by Dolores O'Riordan

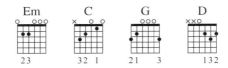

Verse
Heavy Rock beat

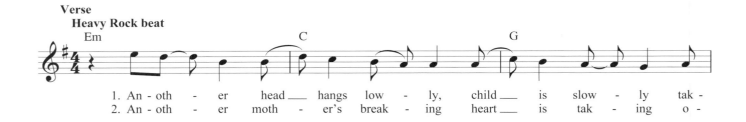

1. An - oth - er head ___ hangs low - ly, child ___ is slow - ly tak -
2. An - oth - er moth - er's break - ing heart ___ is tak - ing o -

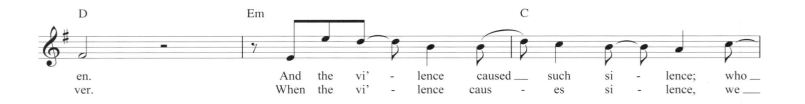

en. And the vi' - lence caused ___ such si - lence; who ___
ver. When the vi' - lence caus - es si - lence, we ___

___ are we ___ mis - tak - en? But, you see, it's not me, it's not my
___ must be ___ mis - tak - en. It's the same old ___ theme since ___ nine -

Pre-Chorus

fam - i - ly. In your head, ___ in your head they are fight - ing ___ with their tanks
- teen six - teen. In your head, ___ in your head they're still fight - ing ___ with their tanks

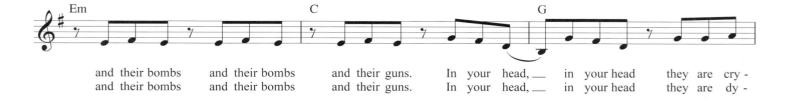

and their bombs and their bombs and their guns. In your head, ___ in your head they are cry -
and their bombs and their bombs and their guns. In your head, ___ in your head they are dy -

Who'll Stop the Rain

Words and Music by John Fogerty

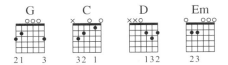

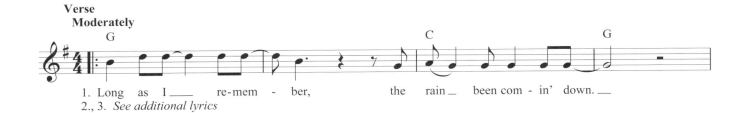

1. Long as I re-mem-ber, the rain been com-in' down.
2., 3. *See additional lyrics*

Clouds of mys-t'ry pour-in' con-fu-sion on the ground.

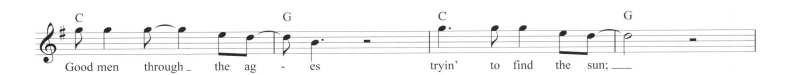

Good men through the ag - es tryin' to find the sun;

and I won-der, still I won-der, who'll stop the rain?

Additional Lyrics

2. I went down Virginia, seekin' shelter from the storm.
   Caught up in the fable, I watched the tower grow.
   Five-year plans and new deals wrapped in golden chains;
   And I wonder, still I wonder, who'll stop the rain?

3. Heard the singers playin'; how we cheered for more.
   The crowd had rushed together, tryin' to keep warm.
   Still the rain kept pourin', fallin' on my ears;
   And I wonder, still I wonder, who'll stop the rain?